WITHIN *the* Wiles *of an* UNCHARTED JUNGLE

A TRUE STORY

A NICARAGUAN PLANE CRASH

1966

by

Gregory Lantz *"TARZAN"* Smith, M.D.

Plastic & Reconstructive Surgeon

DORRANCE
PUBLISHING CO
EST. 1920
PITTSBURGH, PENNSYLVANIA 15238

Cover Design by Troy Robertson.
www.troyrobertson.com

Dorrance Publishing Co
585 Alpha Drive
Pittsburgh, PA 15238
Visit our website at www.dorrancebookstore.com

ISBN: 978-1-6366-1118-1
eISBN: 978-1-6495-7348-3

Dedication: To my beloved wife, "*Rapunzel*," without whom there could be no "*magic*."

CONTENT

Preface

To be found within these pages is the story of how it came to be I acquired the persona of *"TARZAN,"* how the idea of synchronicity affected my life, and how I discovered the secret of true love brought by a series of synchronicities and concatenations. Entwined within all this, is culminated a harrowing plane crash within the midst of an uncharted jungle where disease and death are expected, and escape is not assured...

SYNCHRONICITY

Carl Jung, a psychiatrist, recognized a phenomenon he called synchronicity. By *"synchronicity"* he recognized highly, astronomically improbable coincidental sequential events originating as *"acausal"* thought (dreams, desires, fantasies – all intangible) on occasion culminate in causal reality (become real; become tangible). If this phenomenon is recognized it lends a hint of omniscient guidance in an otherwise phlegmatic universe...

Part I

The BEGINNING

My need to morph into the persona of *"Tarzan"* came by observing Mother and by the encounter of a life altering movie...

CHAPTER 1

MOTHER

Mother had been met early in her life by the tragedies teenage girls encounter when they have no parental guidance and are forced into maturity far too early. By age fourteen she'd developed into a state of voluptuous physical femininity well beyond that of the average teenage girl. So unusually attractive she'd become, every man that saw her became obsessed with her.

So, it should be no surprise, at fourteen, she was impregnated by her high school "*sweetheart*." They "*married*." I was born. Immaturity and inexperience led to their divorce shortly thereafter.

Her fate, whatever it may have been, changed. Now she was a teenage girl divorced and burdened with a kid ~ me. She dropped out of high school and became a "*ticket girl*" at a movie theatre. Not yet capable of economic independence, "*we*" were forced to move back into Grandma's house within the dregs and dearth of the Kansas City "*ghetto*."

Despite Mother's obvious destitute state, her secondhand clothes, her unappealing prospect of having a kid tag along on dates, it seemed not to distract the barrage of men that tried to win her favor AND impress me.

Realizing the sacrifice mother had made to bring me into this world, I was determined to become what she thought a man ought to be by observing the men she dated.

During her early teenage years, my adolescent Mother had an exclusive attraction toward professional "*body builders.*" Encounters with these men came without effort. All she need due is "*hang out*" in her bikini at the local swimming pool where these men came to tan.

As she "*matured,*" Mother became disenchanted with "*body builders.*" She worried their interests were too narrow and that they would not have the capacity to raise me to my "*full potential.*" She began to seek men of "*intellect.*"

But by the time she had begun to seek men of intellect, I'd already been "*indoctrinated*" into believing, were I to grow into a "*scrawny*" man, a woman such as Mother could never be attracted to me. So, at that point in my development, ingrained within a part of my personality, was a desire to become as muscular as the men she'd dated.

The prevailing "*apocryphal*" societal platitude in the 1940's was that men of "*brawn,*" by attempting to develop the "*perfect physique,*" must "*sacrifice*" their intelligence at the altar of "*Big Muscle.*" On the other hand, men of "*intellect,*" the guys that were "*scrawny*" by comparison, had excessive amounts of time, due to their unattractiveness, to develop their brains toward a broader variety of interests. It was believed a man could not be both muscular and intelligent...

Young and precocious but puerile, mother accepted this social platitude. She abandoned her pursuit of muscular men and began to date "*scrawny*" men (But, by so doing, she denied her incontrovertible desire to be with men of physical attractiveness).

Within my third year of life, mother had met a "*smart but scrawny sailor*" that "*fit*" the profile of "*intelligent men that make good fathers.*" He was a "*four-eyed,*" recessive jawed, skinny, unathletic, bony Navy medic stationed in Oakland, California. She met him at a dance. And, of course, he was immediately smitten by her "*rhythmic movement*" and her appearance. She felt this sailor to be the "*perfect*" man "*smart enough*" to raise me and meet her need for "*intellectual*" stimulation. But I knew she didn't exhibit the same flair of attraction she'd had with other suitors. Mother's "*sexual*" attraction to the "*sailor,*" having watched her with other men, from a kid's point of view, seemed to be missing.

The sailor and Mother married. My new "*father*" adopted me. When his service to America as a Navy medic ended, we moved to Missouri and initially stayed at Grandma's house. After obtaining GI funds offered from his years in the Navy, we were "*rich enough*" to leave Grandma's house and move to a modest home built at the edge of a hilly Missouri "*Ozarkian*" woodland. It sat at the furthest advance of a moraine deposited from the last Ice Age. Huge limestone boulders were strewn throughout the topography of the hills that rose beyond an abandoned cornfield that grew behind our house. "*Dad*" entered college and majored in pharmacology hoping this path would allow him to enter medical school. He also took a part time job. Mother began work as a "*laundry girl.*" I began first grade...

I humbly submit, by age six, since "*Dad*" thought his highest achievement would be to become a doctor, I too believed I should aspire to become a doctor. I felt this would prove to Mother I was as smart a kid as she'd hoped I'd be. With the help of my "*Dad,*" I also began studying science...

Unfortunately for Mother, by the time I'd reached my sixth year of life, her love for the smart skinny guy, my Stepfather, was fading. It was clear to anyone, including me, mother had become unattracted to him despite his intelligence and his dedication to me.

Mother began to fantasize about finding a man smart, muscular, tall, ruggedly handsome, romantic, and devoted. It would be this man, if ever found, that I began to realize would satisfy her desperate need for "*true love.*" No less a man could ever be her "*soulmate.*" No less a man could she respect. Married to a man that did not fulfill her desires and having failed ever to meet such a man, left her **VERY** despondent...

The MOVIE

In a dented, rusted, cracked chassis 1948 Chevy mother took me to the **UPTOWN THEATER.** It sat at the zenith of a hill in the middle of downtown Kansas City, Missouri. **I was six. It was 1953...**

Swinging her hips to such an extent it threw me off balance as I held her hand, she brought me to the entrance of the theatre. Emblazoned upon gold-plated metal; encircled by a sea of bright amber lights, the theater's marquee read: Now Showing: *"Tarzan & His Mate."*

We entered the theatre. We sat in plush red velvet seats center row not far from the stage.

The auditorium was almost empty. An echoic tune whispered throughout but soon there was abject silence. The lights dimmed. None but an occasional cigarette flair, a cough, a whisper indicated we were not alone...

The drone of a movie projector then revved to shed a beam of light into the darkness onto the massive curtain in front of me. Dust particles and cigarette smoke came alive and danced within the beam. The massive curtains began to hiss and parted to reveal a lustrous silvery screen...

There began a primal musical composition gradually crescendoing. Its resound began echoing throughout the chamber of the theatre. Kettle drums lent a libidinous atavistic beat injected by hedonistic aboriginal cries. *"Cannibalistic"* guttural congas rose in intensity to reveal their repetitive repertoires. Then the wanton sounds of flutes, bassoons, and oboes blended into the beat to mimic the lascivious voices of the forest dwellers. A melee of creatures I'd never before seen danced across the screen ~ elephants, zebras, rhinoceri, hippopotami; crocodiles...

A bold title appeared: *"Tarzan and His Mate "*...written by Edgar Rice Burroughs...starring **MAUREEN O'SULLIVAN** as *"JANE"*... and...**JOHNNY WEISSMULLER** as *"TARZAN..."*

I did not know it then, but this movie was a rerun originally released in 1934. It was 1953 when I first saw the movie. But I did not see it in its entirety for certain scenes, an infamous nude scene that revealed *"Tarzan & Jane" "frolicking wantonly"* within the waters of a botanical paradisical lagoon, had been deemed *"too explicit sexually"* to be viewed. It had been censored. I did not see the uncensored version until 1986 ~ a time when such *"frolicking"* was deemed not sexy enough!

As the celluloid film's reel thinned, it revealed a world of wonderment, of adventure; of romance; a world that unfurled into my reality...

I saw a man named *"TARZAN."* He was feral, rugged, brave, athletic, adventurous, and romantic. He was a man whose gymnastic skill had chiseled him into a being of superior strength; a man that had insight into and empathy for the autochthonous creatures of his world; a man that had won, by the charisma and character of his personality, the immutable love of *"Jane."*

He was the *"idealized"* man for whom I'd heard Mother opine. I knew if ever Mother met a man such as *"Tarzan,"* a man both strong AND intelligent, it'd be he that'd bring her true happiness. I felt, were I to emulate *"Tarzan's"* fictionalized, idealized character, I'd be a son Mother would have been proud to have given birth.

That movie also made it clear to me I did want NOT to live as I'd witnessed the life of mother. I did not want to spend my life lonely and unhappy or strapped to a mate I thought was inadequate. I felt, were I to mature into a man *"Tarzanesque,"* my best shot at finding *"true love"* would be most possible...

So...I set about to become the avatar of *"TARZAN..."*

CHAPTER 2

The VINE of IMMINENT PERIL

Had Mother not married the "*sailor-pharmacist*," had we not moved from Grandma's house to the Ozarkian forest, had I not seen "*Tarzan & His Mate*," my story would have ended here. If none of those synchronous events, one to the next, had NOT happened, I would have led a far more cautious, featureless, painless life. I would have lived a life devoid of romance and adventure. Had I not begun the quest to become the avatar of "*Tarzan*," I would not have found myself caught, many years later, within the peril of an anthropophagic jungle...

When I saw "*Tarzan and His Mate*" I had just begun first grade. The movie so affected me; I began plotting how I could mold myself to become "*Tarzanesque*." I began this odyssey by attempting to achieve "*Tarzan's*" most spectacular feat: swinging from vines!

I'd wandered several times into the Ozarkian forest behind my house searching for a vine from which to swing ~ like "*Tarzan*." But I'd discovered I was far too weak to accomplish this feat. I needed to become stronger. I needed to learn how to climb such things but in a safer less dangerous environment than could be found within a forest. I was at an impasse...

Unrealized by me then, I would soon experience a synchronicity ~ an acausal intangible thought brought to causal tangible reality...

I entered first grade. Shortly thereafter, my classmates and I were introduced to the gym to play dodgeball. Within that gym, I spotted ropes and poles hanging from its ceiling. I realized the ropes and poles were similar to the vines I'd sought to climb except they'd been con-fined to a "*safer*" environment. I knew, were I to practice climbing these gymnastic accoutrements, I'd get stronger and better skilled at the task. Getting stronger by lifting weight, that is, my weight, I knew was a thing that occurred having remembered the bodybuilders mother had origi-nally dated.

From that first visit to the gym onward, despite ropes and poles being forbidden to first graders and, if climbed, would incur punishment by paddle board, I'd sneak into the gym with the intent to become skilled at that task until I could conquer its difficulty; until it'd enhance my strength enough I could return to the forest where the real vines grew!

During first grade, I barely could climb more than a few feet, but, within a few months, I was climbing to the rafters high enough to "*tap*" the ceiling! By second grade I was confident I could "*tackle*" any vine in the Ozarkian forest.

I ventured into the forest to find my "*perfect*" vine...

After several months, I came upon a huge boulder inclined forty degrees that had tumbled and precariously wedged itself into the earth. Standing before it, I felt flea-like in stature. Out from a crack carved deep within the boulder, I spotted a thick, gnarly vine spiraling into the atmosphere. Up, up it went into the arms of a giant oak that held its tendrils far above me. I estimated, were I to prepare it for *"swinging,"* it'd send me greater than one-hundred feet above the ground below.

I tested my grip against its wood. It was perfect. I tested whether it could hold my weight without being torn from the great oak from which it hung. Even bouncing up and down on it caused no untoward effect. I cut loose the vine from the stony crack from whence it emerged and hesitantly tested the arc of its swing by venturing beyond the precipice of the rock. The vine was *"perfect!"*

Having found this vine, I devised a plan I thought might bring me *"Tarzanic glory"* from my elementary school classmates.

I began to brag to the kids at the school my ability to swing fear-lessly out from a cliff ~ like *"Tarzan."* Most were VERY skeptical; some were disgusted by my lack of humility; some were set to be jealous if my bravado proved true.

Having boasted about this feat for several weeks, virtually the entire second grade class had been enticed enough to follow me into the forest.

As the kids lined up at the base of the mountainous boulder, I *"the-atrically"* climbed the precipice of the stone. For dramatic emphasis, before I grasped the vine, I first stood a moment looking circumspectly out over the valley, down to where a distant cornfield grew; down to the ground beneath my feet where all the kids stood. Then, I grasped the vine and took it to the highest point opposite the stone's precipice. I leapt up on the vine to gain height and dashed over the *"skullcap"* of the massive boulder. I did not allow myself extra grip by wrapping my legs about the vine ~ it would not have been *"manly."* I clung to the vine only by the strength of my grip.

Out past the enclosure of forest limbs and leaves I flew, out into a thinning of the atmosphere; out further than ever before I'd gone! During the swing I let out the apish cry of Tarzan: *"Ahhhhh- Ee-Ahhhhh-Ee-Ahh-Ee-Ahhhhhhhhh...!"* Even as the wind swept fiercely past my face, I could hear the kids below gasping with astonishment.

The acceleration of the pendular swing increased my weight far greater than ever before I'd experienced. The *"tug"* was so severe my fingers began to unravel from the vine. At the height of the arc, a hundred feet above the ground, I became weightless but only briefly. Though my arms had developed an intolerable ach, during that moment of weightlessness, I regripped the vine.

The pendulum began to retrace its path. On the way back, as I approached the stone, I heard a *"cap pistol"* snap! The vine jerked into a descent that'd soon impale me against the stone's jagged edifice. Seeing my circumstance had devolved and that I might be bludgeoned into a bloody pulp, the kids ran off...some of them screaming in terror!

The vine continued its descend as I approached the boulder. I reasoned I should hang on to it for as long as possible until the descent would be low enough the fall might not be too harmful. That was my plan, but it failed. The vine became completely untethered at forty feet above the ground. I had to let it go.

Into a mound of scree and saprolite I landed feet first. The momentum crushed me to my knees and shoveled me into the ground. A cloud of dirt burst into the air. My waist bent forward and drove a sharp rock to strike directly between my eyes.

Shaken, a bit unbalanced, dazed, I rose from the incident feeling embarrassed but TRIUMPHANT. Proudly, I began the journey back to my home…

The SCAR

As I broke free from the forest and entered the cornfield, I began to sense a burning sensation and a blurring of my eyesight. I felt wetness between my brows. I reached a hand to feel what I assumed was excessive sweat. Instead, I felt a "*gooey*" fissure separating the continuity of my skin. Pulling my finger away, staring at it, I suddenly realized the wetness was **BLOOD**.

I found my mother in the kitchen washing dishes. By then, I had become so drenched in blood the extent of the wound itself was buried in a thick layer of coagulum. I tugged at Mother's dress. Thoroughly annoyed, she looked down to see me. Stupefied, she drew a finger to my forehead and brought it to her face…

She broke into a hysterical fugue! She ran about the house screaming, mumbling, crying, swearing, and pounding her chest. I thought to
laugh it was so odd. But I dare not. I knew she wasn't running about
the house for my entertainment.

My "*sailor-pharmacist*" stepfather sped home from the university he
was attending and drove mother and me to the nearest emergency
room. En route, mother spit unfair invectives toward not only me but
also my "*Dad*." We were silent and subservient as her rant continued
without a pause for breath...

Unbeknown to Mother, I felt I was not a "*failure*." I felt my adventure was a success. I was certain no other kid would have been brave
enough to do what I did; no other kid would have figured how to time
the landing with the least amount of injury. And the event had made
wise my knowledge about vines and the stresses of gravity. It wasn't
really my fault a stone was in the wrong spot at the wrong time at the
end of my misadventure.

But I knew Mother. I dared not hint my pride. I dared not do anything less than maintain a posture of obedience and solemn regret for
being so "*careless*" and "*stupid*."

It was during this car ride the "*seed*" of becoming a future plastic
surgeon was planted. During the entire time we sat imprisoned by the
confinement of the car, mother had emoted how "*awful*" faces appeared
that have been scarred. Such a blemish on an otherwise perfect face
she attested was "*ruinous*" (I never forgot her words.).

At the emergency room, my "*dad*," now thoroughly besot by anger, pulled up to the entrance, got out of the car, and...walked home!

Mother took me into the emergency room. An authoritative man brought me to a padded table, bent over me, and empathetically asked me to "*be brave*." I knew that phrase. It was the mantra of my mother. The first time I heard mother ask me to "*be brave*," I was three years old. We still lived at Grandma's House:

> Grandma's neighborhood had once been a decent place for people to live but it had decayed into a "*ghetto*." It was no longer safe to live there. We lived there until I was five. Abject poverty accrued by Mother's hapless pregnancy with me meant we were too poor to live anywhere else. Grandmother at least kept us fed and sheltered.
>
> I had wandered into a dilapidated concrete overgrown alley strewn with broken glass and debris that ran a crooked path behind Grandmother's house. I was searching for something with which to play.
>
> I spotted five or six older kids hovering around a trashcan obviously burning something within it. They were laughing and having great fun. I thought to join them.
>
> As I approached the trashcan, I heard a horrible sound ~ the cry of a kitten. I rushed to the barrel to see a kitten lit to flames burning to its death. I grabbed it and ran. Despite their chase, I managed to escape the

miscreants. I returned to Grandma's house and tried to revive the kitten. I held it in my lap; I petted it; I gave it milk. It drank...but soon...it died. The kitten's death crushed my heart...

A week passed...

On a warm day, I had been playing in a vacant lot across the bitumen street from Grandma's house. A girl I'd thought was beautiful had befriended me and had become my *"girlfriend."* She lived in an apartment nearby. We sat playing with some new toys her mother had given her. My Mother sat on the wood railing of Grandma's porch watching our play...

A big kid carrying a BB-gun came toward us. I recognized him. He was the tallest of the kids who had burned the kitten. He stared at me with anger. He cocked his gun and fired a pellet into my chest. I stood. I looked over at Mother. She shouted my name with a nod and pointed at the big kid. She sternly said, *"BE BRAVE!"*

I knew I couldn't beat this kid in a fight and, oddly, it was not within me to hurt him. I thought my best response would be to walk away back to Grandma's porch. As I walked toward Mother, across the vacant lot, across the broken concrete slabs of the sidewalk, across the black tar street, all the way to Grandma's porch, the big kid kept hitting me with pellets from his BB-gun.

I didn't want to humiliate Mother. I did not run. I did not cry. As the bullets pelted my jeans to impart excruciating, bruising pain along the length of my legs and buttocks, I looked only to Mother and the sanctuary that'd be mine once I reached Grandma's porch.

As I finally reached Grandma's porch, I could see Mother beamed with pride. There were tears in her eyes and an expression of compassion as she looked down at me.

Then she looked up...

The big kid was still taunting a reprisal with a big arrogant smile on his face. He waved his BB-gun in defiance and triumph.

He was as big as my mother. But I knew something he did not know. She was as strong as nails and as tough and mean as anyone ever born. I knew her penetrating stare at that kid was a prelude to his utter destruction. I'd seen that stare before.

There came an intense pause. The big kid no longer taunted. He no longer held high his weapon. I knew that kid sensed he'd done something he was about to regret...

Mother shot out from the porch and was upon him before his stunned arrogance had time to recover. She took his BB-gun and smashed it beyond repair. She beat him not with slaps but with her fists until his face bled. Standing over him, she gruffly cautioned, *"Do that to my kid again…and…I'll kill you!"*

He limped off. I never saw him again.*

Yes, I'd heard mother say, *"be brave"* a thousand times. So, when the doctor asked me to *"be brave,"* that's exactly what I did. I did not move; I did not wince; I did not cry. He numbed my cut, cleaned me up, and repaired the fissure between my brows. I'm certain I sustained a scar far less noticeable than had I behaved otherwise.

The *"Vine Catastrophe,"* rather than wither my desire to emulate the *"apeman's"* persona, solidified my belief emulating the feats of the fictional *"Tarzan"* was not beyond measure within the real world. The *"Vine Catastrophe"* rooted the embryonic seed that would germinate into all aspects of my life.

---

* **NOTE**: In today's world I realize some people might conclude my mother had been unkind to me or too stern in expecting me to *"be brave."* But, even then, at three-years-old, I felt extreme pride in myself because of her. I felt the glory of being brave. Had she pampered me, perhaps the real world would have been much more difficult.

CHAPTER 3

A **STAND** of **TREES**

By my ninth year of life I was called *"Tarzan"* nearly as often as by my Christian name. My harrowing *"Tarzanic"* vine swinging escapades had become *"legendary"* among my fellow grade school kids (at least, that's how I'd perceived it). But I'd never achieved swinging from one vine to the next as did *"Tarzan"* in the movies. This *"inequity"* was about to change...

During the summer, while continuing to perfect the *"art"* of *"vine brachiation,"* I'd climbed a particularly narrow tree trunk I would not have normally climbed. But, attached to that tree was a particularly promising vine that had draped across a pond. I thought I might swing out on the vine and drop into the water beneath. As I scaled the trunk to capture the vine, the tree began to bend; it bent over the pond. There was no need to capture the vine. The tree itself had bent as though it were a vine! I let go of the bent tree trunk and splashed safely into the water. The tree snapped back to its original position. It occurred to me, a tree if of a particular diameter, behaved like a...vine...!

This event would soon lead to a synchronicity. I'd searched the ends of the forest to find a series of vines I could catch one to the next to propel through the woods as had *"Tarzan"* in the movies. But I'd never found such a series of vines. Until that day, I'd never realized a series of trees that could bend as that tree over the pond could behave similar to a series of vines. And, I suddenly realized, if I could find such a grouping of tree trunks, I could emulate *"Tarzan's"* feat not by clinging to vines but by clinging to a series of bending trees ~ a stand of such trees!

Into the most primordial part of the forest I went. But it seemed there were no trees that could serve to let me swing from one to the other for any substantial distance, until, just before I was on the verge of *"giving up,"* I came upon a perfect stand of such trees! They were aligned along the gentle slope of a hill covered by a comforting thick mattress of fallen leaves; they stretched about sixty feet...

I began to test the idea whether I could advance from one tree to the next the entire length of their expanse. At first I managed to advance only a short distance. Day by day I became better; I went further. Eventually I could complete the entire run of the trees.

It then occurred to me I should demonstrate this skill to the kids at school.

As had become engrained within my character, I began a typical hubristic campaign. I proclaimed, especially if girls were present, I could *"swing"* through the trees WITHOUT gymnastic equipment and without vines! I shamelessly bragged I could swing from a stretch of trees, one after the other for a distance greater than sixty feet (Admittedly, it seemed sixty feet ~ but I never measured the distance!).

NO ONE BELIEVED ME! In fact, the boast brought mockery and laughter. It didn't matter. I continued my bravado with even greater flair…!

Eventually, as is the usual case for such arrogant "*bragging*," the more competitive boys bid me prove my outrageous bluster or "*shut up*." That day finally came…

Gathering at the edge of the forest, a number of the boys and several girls including a beautiful Italian, brown-eyed girl for whom I'd already "*seriously fallen in love*," followed me deep into the hilly wooded interior of the Ozarks. We came upon the stand of trees.

As I ascended the first tree, the boys began to mock me. They began acting as though they were a troop of chimpanzees. They hooted and howled and grunted and lip-smacked. They fell into a "*bow-legged*" gait and scratched their armpits and the top of their heads. They tried to mimic "*Tarzan's*" wail and the "*gorilla chest clap*." But, their imitations, at least for the yell and the clap, were sorely miserable. To carry off those "*Tarzanic*" impressions required a lot of practice! The girls laughed and giggled and had great fun watching the boys act like chimps. I was unperturbed for I knew, if I didn't fail my boast, they'd all be AMAZED and humiliated by their antics!

With exaggerated theatrical aplomb, I climbed the first of the trees high enough the kids below seemed dwarfed. I called out an authentic "*Ahhhhh-Eh- Ahhhhh-Ee-Ahh- Ee-Ahhhhhhhhh*" and followed that with an authentic mighty "*gorilla chest clap.*" Then, I shot out over the stand of trees, one after the other. Leaves broke loose and drifted down, branches rustled; grunts of primal effort came out my mouth. The trunks howled as each baneful fiber bent to the stress of my weight.

The kids below became muted with astonishment. The entire stand was traversed. I released the last tree ten feet above the ground and tucked into a forward role at I struck the ground. I rose unscathed and genuflected with an utmost cunning smile (as I'd witnessed the face of Errol Flynn in the movies). In general, I was received with accolades from most but not all. The boys who had mocked me with the greatest histrionics walked away disheartened and dejected. The girl I'd hoped to impress most, the brown-eyed Italian girl, was elated...and...charmed...

For a week afterward, throughout the school, the tale of that "*performance*" was heralded. As I walked the hallways, I feigned modesty, but I felt heroic.

By ten years old, within the narrow confine of the school hallways, I'd demonstrated enough skill to be referred to as the "*Ozarkian Tarzan.*" When someone heard, "*Ahhhhh-Eh-Ahhhhh-Eh-Ahh-Eh- Ahhhhhhhhh,*" they knew it was me. When the resound of a "*gorilla chest clap*" echoed the hallways, no one had to ask or wonder from whom it came…!

Postscript
Never again, though I'd often searched, did I find another stand of such trees. Years later, returning to my childhood neighborhood in search of that original patch, I discovered the forest had been cut away to make room for houses and a concrete road…

CHAPTER 4

The **OLD WOODEN BRIDGE**

After the "*Stand of Trees*" incident I continued to search adventurous "*Tarzanic*" novelty to be found within the Ozarkian forest.

Behind my house, beyond the cornfield that grew to the edge of the forest where I'd swung from numerous vines, within a narrow chasm tucked at the summit of those hills, there existed a set of railroad tracks that ran beneath an antiquated wood bridge.

The bridge itself crossed vertiginously high above the tracks. Cars could drive over the thing, but the drive was fraught with danger. The wood planks of the bridge were worn thin, and some were missing. The side railings could not be trusted. The timbers of the bridge would vibrate and rattle with menacing intensity each time a car crossed over it or a train passed beneath it.

On a day dreary with fog so thick it made dripping wet the entire forest, I'd hiked through the woods, as I'd done many times before, until I came to the chasm over which that rickety old bridge had been built. I slid down a dirt slope into a gutter on either side of the chasm and worked my way to the railroad tracks. What light filtered from the sun gave muted sparkle upon the wet steel of the track, the ditch, the stones; the wood. Balancing on one of the track's steel rails, I *"tightroped"* toward the bridge. I was **eleven-years-old...**

The bridge had never been more than a *"marker"* to find my way home for it could be seen from a great distance. But this day it presented differently. It'd become a behemoth half-buried in the gloom of fog that might be worthy of a *"Tarzanesque"* challenge. As I looked at that rickety bridge, it occurred to me it might be possible to climb it, a distance of several hundred feet, form the tracks upward to its railing. So, I climbed it without misadventure.

It then occurred to me; a brown-eyed, pony-tailed girl for which I'd been enamored for several years might be impressed were she to see me climb that archaic trestle. I plotted a picnic for the two of us at the bridge with the intent to reveal my daunting prowess by having her witness the harrowing climb of its timber. The plot finally materialized. A month after the initial climb, I convinced this mischievous Italian *"femme fetal"* to accompany me to the bridge for a *"picnic."*

For a while, we played directly beneath the narrow cut of dirt at the base of the bridge's deck...

As I plotted to steal a kiss from her lips, I began to notice a field of inverted conical pits of sand stretched just beyond the tips of our toes. I knew their purpose: These conical pits were meant to bring death to any bug that slipped into them. They were the *"pits"* created by ANT-

LION larvae ~ ugly, bristled, fat, bloated, giant-jawed, black-eyed bugs that eventually metamorph into the beautiful, delicate LACEWING.

To impress this girl, a girl for whom the embers of *"innocent"* love had been ignited, I pointed to the pit. I delivered a soliloquy about the ant. The full-lipped, brown-eyed girl seemed in awe my knowledge. Since our *"picnic"* was almost at its end, I thought it the perfect time to impress her by showing her the courage I could exhibit by climbing the bridge.

She held little conviction my *"capabilities"* and giggled with shame her disbelief in my boast. I let her bemuse herself long enough to let her *"skepticism"* come to full fruition and, therefore, make even more spectacular the achievement…if I pulled it off…?

I dramatically hopped over the banister of the bridge and descended along its wood beams with *"gorilla"* strength and agility until I reached the ground below.

From the tracks at the base of the bridge, I could see my wanton Italian leaning over the precarious railing with an expression of profound incredulity. Her ponytail had fallen forward across her shoulder. For reasons I'd yet to understand, the very sight of her, her ponytail, her eyes, her expressions drove me mad with a desire I could only fathom MUST be love.

On my ascent back to the top of the bridge, it seemed my boyhood doughtiness had impressed her. She beamed with joy, she clapped, she hopped up and down; her ponytail whipped back and forth. When I arrived at the very top of the bridge intent to reward myself by tenderly compressing her lips into an evancalous kiss, I first cried out: "*Ahhhhh-*

Ee-Ahhhhh-Eh-Ahh-Eh-Ahhhhhhhhh" followed by a *"gorilla chest clap."* And, with that, I lost my balance.

Off the bridge I fell. As her image diminished in perspective, *"BE BRAVE"* came to mind. I kept my dignity. I did not show fear. I made no sound. Then my lights went out.

For a time, indeterminate, I lived as though asleep. No thought came to my head. I was consumed by a warm, tranquil sensation..

I began to hear a far off, distant, almost imperceptible worried, tearful call of my name. At first, I did not recognize the voice, but, as I recovered, it became increasingly clear the voice was that of my girlfriend.

I looked about. I found myself cradled in the dirt of the slanted decline of the valley still well above where the railroad tracks ran. I had fallen on a dirt concavity on either side of two Pleistocene boulders. By the *"Grace of God"* my rout back to the top of the bridge had brought me closer to the slant of the chasm well above its deepest recess. Despite having been *"taco shelled"* between two massive boulders, I'd not struck either rock. It was the jarring effect of striking the dirt that had ricocheted my brain within its encasement that brought me to momentary *"black out."* I felt that, having not encountered all the things that could have killed me, bespoke the providence of God....

Shaking off my initial disequilibrium, I returned to the top of the bridge. I could see the girl cared about me ~ maybe *"loved"* me. She was crying She'd thought me dead...

Our *"date"* ended with one last kiss at her doorstep...

Part II

A LOVE QUIXOTIC

As if an immutable, indelible script had been written within the nascent fiber of the universe, there occurred a miraculous incontrovertible series of events, one to the next, that led me to my first encounter with true consummate love and, ultimately, to an adventure that should have ended my life...

CHAPTER 1

The *FEMININE VESTAL of* **IRISH DESCENT**

I'd arrived at my fifteenth year of existence. I'd searched but not found *"true love."* But then, I came upon a feminine vestal of **Irish** descent...

I was in tenth grade *"Junior High."* All the kids of the junior high had been *"bused"* to the senior high gymnasium to listen to a drone about the proper attitude junior and senior kids should have during the final years of their tutelage. On this day, I sat at the highest bleacher of the high school gymnasium ...totally bored.

As I sat waiting for the principal's harangue, adolescent student bodies filled the gymnasium until their overflow was accommodated by a sea of foldout chairs that blanketed the entire basketball court beneath me. Amidst a cacophony of inflective pubescent voices, heads bobbed and twisted and turned, rubber band rockets and paper airplanes sailed through the stagnant air and playful rough housing broke out here and there.

Though it was spring, the day was warm, too warm! The school, as was the case for most schools in that day, had NO air conditioning. The gym had become insufferably hot and steamy despite open windows and fans. My boredom had become intensified by the inescapable confinement imposed. I thought to leave. But my timing was off. The *"principal"* of the senior high came to the microphone and began to speak. Monotone reverberant lethargies came out his mouth as unintelligible *"grownup"* trope and platitude irrelevance. I was approaching the first stage of COMA induced by suffocating intense disinterest.

Just before I fell into complete somnolence, I noticed a focused sunbeam striking through a gymnasium skylight. So curious was the beam; so intensely bright, so spellbound my thought regarding it, none but the beam of light registered. The gym might as well have been totally empty. As I followed this ray of light I discovered it fell onto a head of hair the colors of autumn; a face chiseled to perfect feminine dimension; large eyes; full lips. The light fell upon a girl who sat attentively in a foldout chair in the midst of the basketball court with shoulders and back straight, legs modestly crossed; listening; staring toward the auditorium stage. Though she must have been my age, already she'd blossomed into full femininity. Even her gesticulations, even the movements of her body were as arrows to pierce my heart. She was an anachronism. She did NOT belong in this sea of adolescent idiots. Hers was a femininity quite above the fray, a jewel in a mound of coal. Her image irrepressibly singed my soul.

I felt she was the *"Jane"* for whom I'd been searching…

As I stared at her, it seemed she *"sensed"* the intensity of my captivation. Her expression became one of irritating disquiet. She searched the gym. When her eyes fell upon me her search stopped. With a demure pout and an expression of consternation, she stared back defiantly...

I was confused. What should I do now that we've "*connected?*" Should I continue to look at her or should I look away? Would I offend or thrill her if I continued to look at her? I was too young and inexperienced to know how to handle the moment. Right or wrong, I could not do less than but focus upon her every detail...

The assembly ended. She stood. As she walked away, she seemed puzzled, off balance. She hesitated for a moment and turned back to look one last time at me. And then...she was gone...

My heart could not have pounded with greater intensity...

At the end of the assembly, there was no reality for me but her. I tried to follow her as she left the gym. I plowed down through the bleachers onto the gymnasium floor. Without caution, I ripped past one kid after the next searching the strawberry-blonde of her hair. I flew out into the street where the buses were loading the students and searched every bus window...she was gone!

Several months passed as I tried to find her. Wherever I searched there was no hint she existed. My despair consumed me. Every aspect of my life narrowed to only one need ~ finding her. I knew it was she and ONLY she that could fill the hollowness of my heart; only she that could provide the sustenance to satiate my soul; only she that was the "*girl*" with whom the bliss of "*true love*" could blossom.

I began to believe I'd dreamt her existence…

There came a day my Mother had been invited to have pizza with a neighbor that had recently moved to the neighborhood and lived not more than two blocks away. Her daughter would be with her. I was forced to come along though I had had other plans and protested vehemently.

As Mother and I entered the restaurant, we saw the neighbor with her daughter. The daughter's hair was strawberry-blonde, but I could see nothing else except there seemed an uncertain resemblance to the girl for whom I'd been searching. Too shy to look at this girl directly and positioned at her side at the parlor table too close to sneak a look, we began to eat pizza.

As Mother and her new *"friend"* began talking, there was an unspoken *"magnetism"* between the daughter and I that was overwhelming, alluring; inexplicable. I felt an immense unbearable attraction to her despite not having had anything but the color of her hair to estimate…

This girl, with an enigmatic manner of coquettish innocence, wiped her hand on my thigh rather than use her napkin. Though it was not more than a brief embrace, still, it consumed me with a cataract of passion. Why did she choose my thigh? Was it a sign? Had what I felt seeped into her subconscious so intensely she could not but find this gesture to register I was not alone in my desire? Regardless the reason, despite the terror or my shyness, I turned to scrutinize her features with greater clarity. At that point, I began to realize she was the very same girl for whom I'd been searching.

When she noticed I had turned to look at her, she sensually muttered a phrase too muted to understand. Yet, the sound of her voice was unmistakably that of a seductress oblivious to her attraction; oblivious to her beguiling innocent charm; oblivious to the fact I was totally enamored by her. I no longer doubted this girl **MUST BE** my *"Jane."*

The pizza encounter ended...

Listening to Mother and her newly acquired neighborhood friend, I discovered this girl went to the same junior high I attended. I discovered she was a girl of Irish descent possessed of light green eyes and strawberry blonde hair and the most perfect blend of freckles. I determined it was she I would pursue with the same intensity I'd pursued becoming the avatar of *"Tarzan."* She would become my *"Jane"* whether she knew it or not!

Our romance began…

Within every waking hour I plotted how best to capture her love, how best to engender an irrepressible courtship no girl could reject, how best to create moments novel, romantic, passionate; moments conceived by no other kid but one such as me; moments composed like those encountered within the romantic novels that'd described inseparable love. All other interests I'd once sought had become rarified almost to extinction by this pursuit...

Of the years our courtship flourished, there came realities of romance and adventure set adrift well above the banalities of the mortal existence of teenagers ~ too many to chronicle. I present a night, one of many, of phantasmal bliss:

The Dark of a Stormy Night

Within the dark of a stormy summer night, within the wee hours of morning, I awoke with a start. Looking about, confused, apprehensive as though a premonition had entered the atmosphere of my room, I discovered I was completely alone. And yet, I felt something or someone beckoning me. I lifted the window near my bed and peered out its screened aperture. Streetlights radiated through a mist brought by a drizzly rain ~ the lights seemed alive as their intensities expanded and shrank within undulations of shifts in the precipitous wind. The bitumen street at the front of my house stretched out as a scintillating piceous wave beneath the lights. Inexplicably, I felt compelled to leave my room. I lifted the screen, I tumbled down to the ground, and I soon found myself standing in the middle of the street still befuddled by the enigma that had possessed me...

I began to walk not knowing why I'd ventured out from the warmth of my dry bed into the misty wet of this night...

Somehow, not having registered the path I'd taken nor having used my senses to navigate it, I'd found myself standing in the wet grass beneath the balcony window of the girl that'd captured my heart.

How? Why?...

There suffused an aura that portended there would be romance; that portended I would not be alone this night...

Lightning lit the sky. I saw her silhouette standing at her balcony window. Her gown was transparent and shown the curves of her body in a way beguiling to a young man's heart. She was perfect.

Minutes passed...

Another burst of lightning was followed by a torrent of warm rain. She no longer stood at the window to her bedroom but now stood at the screen door to her rec room, a room that led directly to the backyard where I stood. I walked toward her. She opened the screen door. Without a word spoken between us, I cradled her in my arms and carried her to a nearby hillock of tall thick grass. I laid her in the pillowy softness of its bed. We kissed passionate endless kisses, kisses that stretched well into the night...

As the hint of dawn came, I lifted her once again into my arms and carried her back to the rec room door. As she returned to that room, she turned and pressed herself to its screen. We once again embraced allowing our lips and bodies to crush against its metal.

I returned home…

The STEPFATHER

The love between me and the feminine girl of Irish descent was blackened by the presence of her Stepfather. As I came to know him, I began to realize he was a wicked, cowardly alcoholic with villainous, lascivious intention toward his Stepdaughter. So immaculate was her flawless beauty, most men could not control their libidinous desire. I knew her Stepfather plotted to deflower her. I was in his way. He hated me!

Though initially she lived but two blocks from me, her Stepfather's covetous desire for her made it almost impossible for me to court her without burden. In a way, her stepfather's constant attempt to intervene between she and I intensified greatly our desire to become inseparable. For this reason, my courtship of this beauty compelled me to create adventurous assignations far greater than otherwise would have been necessary:

The BARN

On February 14th, Valentine's Day, within six months of having fallen incontrovertibly in love, I'd conspired to be with my *"Jane."* It would be a special day. I'd regail her with novel romantic adventure not typical of the platitudes practiced by most teenage suitors who'd confessed their love. But it was not to be!

Her Stepfather announced she could not spend the day as she had planned. She could **NOT** be with me. The family was ordered to accompany the Stepfather to the stable where they kept their horses. They would be there the entire day. In addition, he **FORBADE** me to see her, to call her, or to write to her...

I was defiant...!

After receiving the Stepfather's heartbreaking "*news*," I came to the slant of the bitumen street at the front of his house. I pulled from my pocket a complete palate of colored chalk. Upon the streets cracked surface, I drew a twelve foot red heart pierced by a white arrow. I wrote: **I'll Love You Forever. I drew our initials within the heart**. I then left...

Knowing the path the family took to attend the horses, I hid behind a giant oak that'd allow me to sight the barn and the family's arrival at the stable...

I was prepared to stay hidden behind the tree the entire day if necessary but shortly after I'd settled behind the huge oak, they drove past it toward the barn.

Immediately, I advanced to a vast cornfield athwart the barn. The field had not been sewn but it had been plowed. Accumbent, within the grooves of the field, I plowed through the mud until I arrived at a barbed fence just shy of the barn. When it seemed safe, I hoped over the fence and came with silent stealth to the edge of the barn ~ an edge that could not be seen by the family. I "*abraded*" my way along its dilapidated grey wood until I came to its entrance. The barn doors were open. I ran into the barn. I did a gymnastic "*kip up*" into its hayloft and then I hid behind a bale of hay. There I crouched hoping desperately there'd come a moment my "*Jane*" would enter the barn alone...

From a loft aperture, I could see my chaste beauty riding her horse. It seemed she was so intent to ride there might not be a moment she'd venture into the barn. I began to feel great despair. But, similar to the night I'd carried her to a knoll of grass, there emerged a spiritual aura between us we seemed to sense when either of us were near. This day was no different...

I noticed she'd abruptly stopped trotting her horse. She seemed to look about as though confused, as though a thought had perplexed her. She dismounted. She grabbed a "*seed bucket,*" looked about to assure her family were engaged without her, and advanced toward the barn...

I came to the edge of the loft. She did not notice. Her hair was of strawberry gold and bounced wantonly as she came to the stable beneath me...

I *"kipped down,"* turned her about, embraced her tenderly and kissed her. She seemed not startled. She seemed to expect I'd be there. I said, *"I'll love you forever."* And, with that I *"kipped"* back into the loft above. There I hid until dusk; until the family left.

Our Valentine secret remained known to no one but ourselves...

The **PROM** ~ *A Plot Gone Askew*

The Stepfather, in an attempt to sever me from his stepdaughter, had moved from my neighborhood into Illinois. They'd settled in a modest farmhouse outside the skirts of a town that consisted of no more than a post office tucked within vast acreages of corn and wheat. She now lived three hundred miles from me...

Secretly, she'd managed to let me know how to locate her. Many nights I'd drive the 300 miles that separated us and steal her from her bedroom window. We'd be together until early dawn. These interludes continued until our senior year of high school was at its end. Prom night neared...

A week before her prom, my *"vestal virgin's"* Stepfather, suspecting his stepdaughter might be plotting to spend it with me, had forbade her to leave their house. In fact, he intended to lock her in her bedroom until the night of prom had passed.

There seemed no hope we'd find a way to be together...

But then, as though an omniscient benevolence had watched over the two of us, a number of synchronous events concatenated.

During the course of her senior year my *"Jane"* had befriended an English teacher. He had become her confidant. He knew of our impassioned love. He knew her Stepfather's behavior had degenerated into one of lechery. It was thought her Stepfather would soon rape her...

The English teacher felt compelled to concoct a plan that might deceive the Stepfather into allowing my *"Jane"* to go to the prom. She and the English teacher enticed a high school boy, slavishly infatuated with her, to pretend to be her prom date. The Stepfather had never had jealousy of this boy. He changed his mind and decided he'd allow my *"Jane"* to be taken to the prom if it were this boy that'd be her date. But that was not the intent of my *"vestal virgin,"* the English teacher nor myself!

Prom night, the high school boy met my *"Hibernian maiden"* at the Stepfather's house. Instead of driving her to the prom, he drove her to the English teacher's house where I'd been waiting for her. To avoid recognition of my car, the English teacher had me borrow his car to drive to the prom.

In the beginning, all went well...

We danced and laughed as though we were the only two beings on earth...

Toward the end of the evening pictures were being taken on a theatrical stage four feet above the basketball court at the end of the gymnasium. The lights in the gym had been muted but the stage lights had been turned to a glaring brightness. Sitting at the center of the stage floor was a white wrought iron love seat upon which photos were being taken. To be *"immortalized,"* we took our seats at the *"photo bench."* We posed.

As the photographer approached, he suddenly froze. He looked outward from the stage. We followed his eyes as he turned from us. There, at the opposite end of the gym, still standing within the entrance hall, were two backlit silhouettes ~ a male and a woman in tall high heels...

The aura of impending doom was so prevalent, the music was stopped. The riot laughter and dancing ceased. The gym fell eerily silent...

The silhouettes advanced. The clicking sound of the woman's high heels malevolently intensified and echoed. The sea of teenagers parted as the silhouettes approached the stage.

Light from the stage first fell to the feet of the adults as they came nearer. It crept upward until their faces were fully lit. Before us there stood my *"vestal virgin's"* Mother and Stepfather. The man looked angry; he looked inebriated; he smelled of cigarette smoke. The mother looked bitter and disgusted. They had discovered our ruse...

For a prolonged intensity, there was no movement; no sound. The Stepfather then shot up to the stage, grabbed his Stepdaughter's shoulder with such force it ripped her gown, and slung her to the floor. The impact busted her lip. She began to bleed.

I became **ENRAGED**! As the stepfather threateningly leered above his stepdaughter, I grabbed his suit lapels, lifted him off his feet, and carried his despicable "*jellyfish*" body until it slammed against a brick wall at the corner of the stage. There he dangled helplessly while I slammed him again and again against its wall. Through clenched teeth and a scowling face I told him no man, not even God, could prevent his Stepdaughter's destiny. She and I would not, we could not EVER be separated! He needed to "*give up!*"

I felt a hand grab my shoulder. It was a policeman. With gun drawn and cocked, he instructed me to let go this man. I released the Stepfather. He crumpled to the stage...

The policeman spun me around and dropped me to the floor simultaneously cuffing my arms behind me and pressing a knee against my neck. He had a partner. The partner asked the stuporous stepfather whether he wanted me arrested and jailed.

For reasons I've never understood, the stepfather said, "*No. Just make the kid promise to leave town tonight and never return.*"

In defeat, I promised I'd follow that directive. As I still lay cuffed, the stepfather, my Irish auburn-haired girlfriend, and her mother exited the gymnasium through its back door. The two adults got in the front seat of their car and threw my bleeding "*date*" into its back seat. The Mother took off her high heel and began beating her **bloodied** daughter with its spiked end as they drove off and disappeared. Seeing this, I felt hopeless; I felt unbearable anguish. Tears welled...

My cuffs were removed. Before being escorted from the gymnasium by the policemen, I gathered the corsage that had been torn from my *"true love's"* wrist. Its scent was that of hers, the girl I'd ever desperately loved. I thought it would be the only vestige of her I'd ever know. From that town, forlorn, miserable, tears so welled within my eyes I could barely see, I drove back three hundred miles to my home within the bleak dark of night...

A **PLANE TICKET**

Knowing the strawberry blonde's imminent crisis of rape by her stepfather, the English teacher had not abandoned his effort to help her. He bought her a plane ticket to Kansas City. She contacted me. I was to meet her at the airport...

I was now eighteen; she was seventeen. The year was 1966. We were still considered under the authority of our parents. Our fate resided with them.

Fortunately, Mother had lived a life complicated by love and despair. She knew the girl's caitiff Stepfather's lecherous intent. She needed no convincing to see how adamant her son loved the girl he'd courted from the days of his fifteenth year. She knew my character. She knew I'd not part from the *"strawberry blonde"* regardless the depredation . Already we'd forsaken every comfort. We'd faced starvation and abject poverty. Mother would help us. She'd let us live in her basement...

Inexplicably, the girl's parents made no attempt to separate us...

CHAPTER 2

The Attempted **RAPE** *of* **MOTHER**

It may seem an incongruity to slip this chapter into the narrative but there is good reason for it. My mother had greater compassion for our circumstance not only because she was a forlorn romantic searching for "*true love*," but also because she had great loathing for any man that threatened a girl or woman with rape.

She'd once related a story to Grandma not knowing I was near. It went something like this:

> Mother, still barely an adolescent, had once been accosted by three teenage "*men*" who dragged her into an alley behind grandma's house. She was carrying a bag of groceries that kept her initial defense helpless. The "*men*" savagely tore lose her bag of groceries and began to rip off her clothes. They flung her to the ground. But, unbeknown to them, mother was far tougher than her appearance would indicate. When she

became enraged, her strength became inflexible ~ like steel.

The "*men*" soon realized they'd thrown themselves into a tornado, not of wind but of "*spikes and teeth and nails.*" She pummeled the three of them, bit and scratched them. She poked their eyes and kicked them toward infertility. Their blood splattered, their faces bruised and bloated; their desire wilted. Within a matter of a few brief minutes, two of them lay groaning in the dirt and debris of the alley while the third limped away...

Mother picked up her groceries and returned to Grandma's house essentially disheveled and a bit bruised but nothing more...

In a sense, the history of Mother's misfortune proved an asset to our dire circumstance. It enhanced her desire to keep my "*Jane*" far from the clutches of her Stepfather by letting us take temporary residence in her basement...

CHAPTER 3

The **IRISH Crop Duster**

We two, the *"Tarzan & Jane"* of Kansas City, though madly, incontrovertibly in love, suffered the wretched destitution of two teenagers possessing immutable adoration but no other asset to fend against the inequities of life.

The reality of our predicament soon beclouded our bliss. We needed help greater than my mother could provide...

My **Irish** beauty, shortly after arriving in Kansas City, decided she'd try to contact her long lost genetic Father. She hoped her true Father might be compelled to help us. Although her true Father had never been in her life past the first year of her birth, she had never begrudged his absence...and...she'd forgiven him. She'd once told me why she'd been told he'd left the family: Historically, her father had caught his wife, her Mother, in bed with his Brother. He walked away and never returned.

Though she'd never tried to contact her father before, she feared poverty and hardship might separate us. In desperation, although it was probable her father might have no interest in her, she wrote him a letter.

Stunningly, after several weeks, there came a response. He would fly to Kansas City to meet her...and...me...

My girlfriend's father arrived at the Kansas City airport within a few weeks following his response to her letter. As he sauntered past a turnstile, I was stunned by his appearance. It was clear from whence derived the unparalleled, inimitable beauty of my Hibernian "*Jane.*" There came a six-foot-four, "*ginger-haired,*" pale green eyed, white-toothed square-jawed, **Irishman**. His hair was thick and unruly and flared into the variegated colors of a flame. He was muscular and broad shouldered. His mannerisms bespoke the apotheosis of classic masculinity. He impressed as an unscripted archetypical "*Quentin Durward,*" "*Matt Quigley,*" "*Don Juan,*" "*Scaramouche,*" "*d`Artagnan,*" "*Lancelot*" or an "*Ivanhoe*" might impress! But he was **NOT** a fictional character writ by some nerdy novelist on some moldy sheet of paper. He was **NOT** fashioned by some director whose script attempted to give representation of manliness from reels of celluloid "*retakes.*" He was a blood and flesh breathing exemplar of what a man ought to be ~ unscripted and natural! All this man needed to complete his image was an "*Indiana Jones*" hat, a bandolier, a high powered rifle, a machete, and a 44 magnum draped diagonally across his hip (Later, it turned out he owned and wore ALL those things!).

After our obligatory greeting, he began to speak. I was not disappointed. It seemed beneath his "*mantle*" of rugged individualism there was intelligence, creativity, adventure, and romance. He'd been a fighter pilot in World War II and then, a fighter pilot during the Korean War. He'd since become a crop duster the past sixteen years in Nicaragua and, though most crop dusters in Central America die within a few years; his skill was so great he'd never yet been injured.

As I listened to his tales of adventure, as I watched his mannerisms, it became clear to me, if my mother ever met this man, her relationship with my then "*beta male*" sailor-pharmacist stepdad would end. Over the years, I'd heard Mother opine the ideal man she thought could be her "*soulmate*." She'd begun to believe such a man "*did not exist.*" And yet…there he was!

En route from the airport, we were to meet Mother. Mother was a highly intelligent, sybaritic, voluptuous, thick- haired blonde; a translucent green-eyed German seductress that'd enamored any male that saw her. I knew, when Mother and my girlfriend's father met, an irrepressible MAGNETIC attraction would occur. I knew it was the end of Mother's marriage to my scientist Stepfather. I felt sorrow for my Stepfather but happiness for Mother…

During the summer of 1966 my mother became madly in love with the strappingly handsome Irishman. The two of them, profoundly entangled our own relationship by the unsubtle amorous intrigue burgeoning between them.

The SUMMER *of* 1966

During the summer of my eighteenth year of life, 1966, my girl-friend's father, the World War II fighter pilot became aware I'd acquired, by stealth and grandeur, the nickname *"Tarzan."* He knew I'd studied the biota and fauna of the jungles with particular interests in entomology and primatology. He knew I'd long desired to enter a *"true"* jungle to collect bugs and to witness the marvels of its life. He also knew, if granted, I'd channel these interests of science toward becoming a SURGEON ~ the ultimate goal of my life.

Knowing all this about me, having subsequently irrevocably fallen in love with my mother, it is probable he felt compelled to bring me to Nicaragua for a *"free"* month long excursion into the jungle to *"collect bugs."* I'm certain he made this offer to further enhance his prospect of capturing that which he desperately desired~ Mother's consent to *"run away with him."*

It was the month of August this offer was made. But there were caveats to his offer he felt I should consider before accepting it. He warned, during the month of August in Nicaragua, the jungles were beset constantly by *"buckets"* of rain so thick *"you could hardly breath."* He warned Nicaragua was a dangerous place to be. Miscreants of all variety roamed its streets and jungles. If these admonitions didn't scare me and I agreed to take his offer, he'd invite his daughter to come along. We'd stay at his *"hacienda."* It'd be our *"outpost to adventure."*

After a battery of vaccinations, on a TACA twin engine prop plane, we, my *"Jane"* and I, flew to Central America. But the flight was not direct. We rose high into the atmosphere and down again to land in Mexico, then Guatemala, then Honduras, and...finally...in Managua Nicaragua. After a series of tympanic ear membrane altitude "*compressions decompressions*," we'd developed not only temporary hearing loss but also earaches.*

---

*Note: in 1966 Managua, pronounced by the natives, "ma NOW wa," was the capital city of Nicaragua.

Part III

The **ADVENTURES** *of* **NICARAGUA**

CHAPTER 1

MANAGUA

The **MANAGUA AIRPORT**

In 1966 the Managua Airport was not much more than a gutted, sparsely grassed runway plagued by the rusted debris of tragic aircraft cataclysms. Looking out the port of my window onto this butchered field, I clearly saw why so many planes had crashed. To successfully navigate onto the airfield, the pilot had to fly between the tips of massive tropical trees while simultaneously dodging errant electric wires partially camouflaged by vegetation. Were either to be misjudged, the trees or the wires, the plane would catapult its passengers to certain death.

While the pilot swept erratically closer to the ground as he dodged branches and tree trunks and slipped past black electric wires, every fiber of my being was alert with worry! But I controlled the outward manifestation of my fear so that my *"Jane"* saw only the masculine mantle befitting a *"real man."*

Our TACA "*pilot*" hit the tarmac with an impact so startling the aircraft's wheels should have burst free and the wings should have cracked off! We lurched forward striking the seat in front of us and then ricocheted backward to strike the "*cushioned*" steal at our backs. As the plane glid forward, it screeched and rattled and sped far too fast toward the airports hanger...

There came an alarming screech followed by an abrupt halt. Again, we were crushed forward and back! For a moment, afterward, there was austere silence within the plane's cabin. As I looked ahead toward the front of the aircraft, still besot by terror, it seemed the scene before me had become frozen into the unalterable reality of memory...

The plane's exit hatch blew open. As we stepped from the almost vertical ladder, we inhaled a torrid gust of russet dust that layered upon our face and clothes and penetrated our lungs.

Our luggage was indifferently dropped at our side. The plane was rotated, refueled, and reloaded with a throng of Amerindians.

Realizing we stood in an open field of cracked concrete and patches of etiolate grass and were starkly alone without evidence of eminent rescue, we woefully watched the plane rise into the troposphere until it diminished into a black dot; then vanished...

Not far from where we stood rose a malachite jungle known to harbor carnassial and viperous predators...including man. As testimony to the man "*thing*," I'd noted a "*Coca-Cola*" billboard at the edge of the "*tarmac*" that had been "*aerated*" by bullets...

Though that was worrisome, we'd not enough energy to emote our situation for the noonday sun had begun to singe our scalps and shoulders and drench our clothes in sweat. We worried more about thirst and being dehydrated like a raisin than by being eaten by a carnivore or envenomated by a snake or shot to death by a miscreant native.

The day dragged on past noon. No one came...

As our hope dwindled, there appeared a distant titian cloud of dusk billowing into the sky behind the wake of an open aired jeep. It seemed a man sporting flaming red hair was at its wheel! As the jeep neared, we recognized *"Jane's"* father. The jeep spun to a dusty stop at our feet. The giant of a man hoped out. He grabbed our gear, and, after a brief but cordial greeting, he loaded us into his *"clunker."*

From the airport, in his worn and abused jeep, we gnawed our way down paths more suited for carts than for cars. We drove beneath trees and foliage so thick only dappled light penetrated. En route to Managua my paramour's father imparted the *"rules"* we **MUST** obey if we were to survive while spending time with him in Nicaragua. With serious brutish countenance, her father spoke:

> *"This is NOT America. Things are much more dangerous here. The rule of law is weak. You two are white. You speak English; they will know you're American. People here think Americans are too rich. They'll want to rob you. There's great danger in all that if you're not alert."*

He tossed a silver pistol loaded with 0.32 caliber bullets on my lap. Dodging a tree limb, a pothole, and a cow carcass, he continued:

"Put this in your pocket. If you and my daughter wander the streets of the city, I want you to hold the gun in your pocket prepared to shoot it through your pants. If you have to shoot someone, you must make certain they're dead. If they live, they will testify against you, and it will be you who are punished regardless the reason you shot them!"

I then noticed he carried a holstered 0.44 Magnum pistol and a sheathed machete. We were daunted; alarmed. After a dramatic pause, still with stern beastly seriousness, he continued:

"When you're driving this jeep be aware there are NO stop lights. The cars do NOT stick to their lanes and the pedestrians often do not look where they're goin'. If you run over someone, you MUST make certain their injuries are fatal. If it seems they're still alive, it's best to back up and run over them until there is no longer breath. Otherwise, you surely will rot in jail or be killed in some other manner."

For what seemed infinity, no one spoke. We just rattled along the pocked road and took in the dense forest. I began to sense I probably was an insignificant blight too immature, a boy not worthy of this man's generosity (Even though I was certain his generosity was inspired from his enrapture of my mother and had little to do with my worthiness.). He was under great pressure to keep me and my "*mate*" alive for the sake of my mother in a country where unnatural death is too often common…

While I pondered the *"smallness"* of my existence, the *"selfishness"* of my free trip, and the ease with which someone might end my life in this primordial place, the fighter pilot resumed his soliloquy:

> *"Oh," he opined with a jovial smile that erased the austere atmosphere, "Be careful of the food. Don't eat anything that has been cleaned in water ~ especially salads and peeled fruit. Don't' brush your teeth with faucet water and don't drink from any spigot and especially any swimming pool. Only drink bottled water. But check even that water to make certain no impurity is seen. Don't eat meat unless it's well cooked."*

We received no further lectures as we bumped on toward the city...

After an arduous drive, we caught sight of **MOMOTOMBO**, an active stratovolcano that last erupted in 1905. Bilious clouds rose out its caldera. At its foot was a freshwater lake named **Lake Nicaragua**. The Irishman told us it harbored fish normally adapted to saltwater that had been *"trapped"* in the lake while it still had inlets continuous with the sea. The saltwater derived from the ocean eventually became dilute until the lake was essentially a freshwater lake. He said it was the only *"freshwater lake"* in the world that contained *"adapted"* swordfish, tarpon, and BULL SHARKS.* Along the lakes western edge sat **MAN-AGUA**, the capital of Nicaragua ~ our destination.

---

*NOTE: It is no longer true Lake Nicaragua is the only lake inhabited by sharks.

Managua City

In 1966, the city was well hidden within the cup of the jungle and beneath the shadow of the volcano. It snuck up to us before we realized we were in it. It was not a city of modernity. Its buildings were too much like those of *"pirate"* movies. I'd reasoned the town must have been built from old world creative minds, from adventurous artisans, from cruel conquerors; from misfits seeking quick fortunes. It was a city built long ago by men surely erstwhile rotted to bone by misadventure, by parasitic infestation or the infirmity of senility.

The streets were of brick or cobbled stone or of wood plank and straw. A putrid stench of rot, feces, and urine permeated every alley; every avenue; every sidewalk. Rain-filled puddles harbored things that were foul in appearance; things that squirmed; things that wriggled; things that fluttered within gaseous algal blooms. Anachronistic rusted cars built decades past were sparsely strewn along the streets. Mostly, carts driven by horse, mule, or oxen crowded the streets. The *"right of way"* fell to anyone who could command it by foul or fair stealth. There were streetlamps adorned with dented tin shades and clear glass bulbs that emitted faint sallow light at the onset of sunset. They were lit for several hours but soon were cut off to *"conserve the capacity of weak electric grids."* Once darkness consumed the city, kerosene lamps and candles were lit. At night, we were warned another danger came to the city. Carnassial and viperous predators roamed in from the jungle onto the city streets along with their *"apish"* brethren, that is, unprincipled humans...

Hotel Managua

Although our true destination was the fighter pilot's "*hacienda*," as he called it, he made a "*pit stop*" at the moss-carpeted curb in front of the Hotel Managua for a leisurely soft drink and a "*bit of gallopinto*" (rise and beans).

The hotel was patterned in the 17th century Churrigueresque architectural style. It was entered through an "*open-air*" breezeway that led to a flowered courtyard restaurant surrounded by Corinthian columns, hand painted glazed tiles, stucco walls, hooded moldings, and Roman arches. Beyond this passage was a swimming pool tucked beneath a second floor alfresco walkway accessed by ascending a baroque wrought iron staircase. The second floor walkway peeked out to the pool through ornate balusters behind which were festooned heavy aureate teakwood doors that led to the private rooms of patrons. I'd never, at eighteen years old, seen anything so spectacular amongst an otherwise totally impoverished city. The hotel stuck out like a jewel pressed into cow dung!

While we sat there a rain came. Day turned suddenly to night as an isolated angry anvil cumulonimbus cloud came to shroud sunlight and poor its cataract. The torrent lasted only a few seconds. The sun soon returned and, as though no rain had come at all, its hot radiance evaporated the city to total dryness.

The fighter pilot took note our wonderment of this odd sequence of rain. Holding an orange soda in a "*repurposed*" glass bottle he'd already checked for "*bugs*," he casually leaned backward against his chair and began another soliloquy:

"*Yep,*" he sighed, "*It's the rainy season. It's gonna' shower down on us almost every day. The clouds will suddenly roll in on us outta' nowhere, the skies will darken to the dark of night, a veritable deluge of rain will come all at once as though it were the end times of Noah, and then…whoosh!…all gone. Sun, blue skies, heat; steam; dry again as though no rain had come in the first place.*"

There was a dramatic pause (He was a theatrical histrionic character as well as a romantic adventurer ~ all of which I admired.). He sipped his soda, looked about, looked at us, and, with a shrug of his shoulder, he looked toward the veranda above the swimming pool. Staring at the balcony, he continued:

"*Up there,*" he pointed to the veranda above the swimming pool, "*John Wayne jumped off that balcony baluster into that swimmin' pool.*"

"*I couldn't let'em outdo me. So, rather than take the staircase, I jumped up to the baluster from the pool ledge (He was as tall as John Wayne.), pulled myself onto the balcony, and, once I caught Wayne's eye, I did a swan dive into the pool. It wasn't the best dive. I landed on my belly and almost emptied the pool. Although the pain was excruciating, I pretended it hadn't hurt a bit.*

"*The 'Wayne' broke into a laugh so loud the whole place echoed with it. Soaking wet, the two of us sat drinkin' at this very table. He was here filming a movie. He was real; natural; a man's man. I really liked the guy…*"

As he spoke, I couldn't help but look at the swimming pool fantasizing about the scene he described ~ about John Wayne and him. I initially wasn't truly focused on the pool itself for I was concentrating on the narrative of the pilot's adventure with *"the Wayne."*

As though a glaze had been suddenly lifted from my eyes, the pool came into focus! The pool was **NOT** as I'd imagined it! It was, instead, a rancid opaque green, with a thin pellicle nurturing intermittent bubbles spitting through its skin. Its scent could not be mistaken for anything but urine, feces, and the rot of meat. When the Irishman ended his tale of John Wayne, after a venerable pause, I asked, *"You and John Wayne dove into that?"*

He looked down at the mosaic of tiles beneath our feet, shook his head, smiled a wry smile, laughed, looked up at me with incredulity and said:

> *"Well, yes, we dove into that pool. But NOT when the pool looks like that! At the end of the week they empty the thing and pour in fresh water. That's when Wayne and I dove in. But I'm glad you asked. If you can't see to the bottom of the pool or it gets too cloudy with green slime, NEVER get in it. Some of the people around her think it's funny to dump carnivorous fish in the pool when no one's lookin'. I once saw a twelve-foot alligator in that pool. And worse, some people pee and poop in the pool too! So, if it doesn't look crystal clear, stay out of it!"*

With that dire warning, we departed for his *"hacienda..."*

The "Hacienda"

We arrived at the Irishman's bungalow. A white picket fence surrounded the roomy one-story structure. It had a small garden almost hidden in a grotto of blossoming huge tropical flowers. The gabled roof was covered by fulgent aluminum far too bright to look at for more than a quick glance. A one-foot screened gap was present at the top of its exterior walls. He explained this design permitted the flow of air ~ a sort of nonelectrical air conditioning system. His place had a veranda with a white loveseat swing. Inside the hacienda were numerous ceiling fans (a thing not often seen in the temperate clime of Midwestern Kansas City back in the 60's).

As we approached the front door, a 4'10" "*mestizo*" maid (a mixed breed of Amerindian- Caucasian) came to greet us and despotically demanded we hand her our luggage though I thought it weighed far too much for her frame to carry. My considerate supplication lasted one second before she simply grabbed my luggage and my girlfriend's luggage and guided us to a bedroom where she delivered us and the luggage.

The stout brutish maid then guided us through the house. All the accoutrements necessary to survive were there. When the maid finished the "*tour*," she asked, with a malapert expression, "*Anyting else gringos?*"

"*Ma'am,*" I shyly almost inaudibly responded, "*Where do the girl and I sleep? Are we together?*"

"*Ware you tink?*" She nodded with incredulity.

"*I tink,*" I said accidentally mocking her speech, "*dare?*" I pointed to the only bed in the room we were meant to sleep. When I said "*tink*" and "*dare*" she raised a suspicious eyebrow but revealed a knowing smile beneath her austere continence.

"*Yes, gringo boy, DARE!*" she pointed…Then, she said, "*Anyting else?*"

We gestured, "*nope.*" She left.

Although I was eighteen and my amative mate was seventeen and we were not married, the Irishman thought it proper, when two people are in love, that they share the same bedroom ~ a thing not thought "*proper*" in the 60's but the father got no argument from me.

For the first few weeks the month of August, the Irishman's daughter and I lulled about at the hacienda, walked into the city…talked. I was so much in love with her I could have stayed cloistered in the bungalow without ever having left. But the days were punctuated by several very noteworthy adventures:

The **Volcano**

Shortly after we arrived, the veteran fighter pilot of two wars, arranged a flight for us borrowing his "*best friend's*" **red** single engine Cessna. His best friend was named "*Parky.*" He was a 62-year-old 5'8" "*white guy*" married to a 16-year-old Amerindian and the father of two infant children. He, himself, used his plane to carry dignitaries or bring supplies into inaccessible regions of the Nicaraguan "*bush.*"

Piloting Parky's plane, the Irishman decided he'd give us a sample of his aeronautical skills. He flew us over Managua City, over Lake Nicaragua, and up along the slopes of the stratovolcano Momotombo. Showing off, he circled the volcanic rim so close the plane's belly scraped over cobbled knots of piceous igneous rock.

My anxiety rose. I worried the thin metal of the plane's belly might rip apart on some black rocky spike and leave my legs to dangle until they became shredded and torn off. Despite my growing anxiety, I feigned what I hoped was a convincing countenance of fearlessness in front of his daughter.

Just as I began to pride myself with my countenance of bravery, the fighter pilot suddenly brandished a mischievous daredevil grin I knew was not a good omen…

We shot straight through the singe of a sooty cloud spit out Momotombo's gut. Into the pit we flew down toward the fiery glow of its fumarolic steam. Fissures broke along the volcanic crater to reveal incinerate **orange** lava splattering dangerously close to our plane. Above the drone of the plane's propellers, like the breath of a monstrous dragon, the volcano gasped sonorous sighs that sucked oxygen from air and expelled towering flames. As we came deeper into the volcano's pit, it began to "*squeeze*" out the plane's breath ~ to suffocate it! The engine began to sputter and misfire…the propeller began to cut in an out. We suddenly dropped!

I prepared to die…

Despite what seemed certain death, the pilot let loose a roguish laugh and pulled us from danger into the bright blue of the sky...

I relaxed. I let loose the plane's front panel to which I'd been clinging. I sat back in the seat almost serene as I assumed the worst of the pilot's bluster had ended. I looked back at my girlfriend. Although pale as Irish wenches already are, even her freckles were washed out and her skin was set aglow with sweat...

I thought to comfort her, but, before I had a chance, the plane revved again, turned, and began a near vertical nosedive! I turned back to the front panel of the plane and dug deep my nails into it. Through the front cabin window, the slope of the volcano came roaring in until it blotted all else from view save the black stones and their steamy vapors. And then, the plane angled parallel to Momotombo's steep slope so abruptly, so near I almost puked...

We descended dauntingly toward Lake Nicaragua's "*sea*" of sharks as we skimmed a foot above the mountain's angle of repose. Black dust was sent billowing upward past the plane's rear rudder to mark the path of our descent. Down, down, straight down...! The accelerating G-force compressed our bodies, plowed grotesque toothy smiles upon our faces, tugged at our hair, and exaggerated our squints.

I saw the pilot tug vehemently at the joystick to pull us out of the dive. But it didn't budge. His face became stern; his brow furrowed; with great strength, he pulled the stick back. The plane rattled then leveled just in time to skim along the sallow purulent waters of the lake rather than dive into it.

In silence, we flew back to the primal Managua airport…

Before this excursion, I had skeptically wondered whether the purported skills of my *"young lasses"* Father were tales of bravado or empty bluster? Were his boasts fact or fable? After that dexterous flight, there was no doubt. This guy's aeronautical skills were unrivaled. He was the real thing. He was a living non-fictional *"Errol Flynn"* in the flesh with no need for *"re-takes!"*

The **Aqua Azui Lagoon**

In a less frightening excursion, several days later, we drove the jeep to **Aqua Azui Lagoon** ~ a *"prestigious"* Crater Lake resort where all the *"swells"* took their friends. It was a favorite spot of the Dictatorial Somoza family. Athwart towering vertical cliffs of igneous rock, a *"country club,"* a *"boating pier,"* and a *"lush botanical garden"* had been created at the edge of the lake. Unlike the infested, refuse, polluted waters of Lake Nicaragua, the waters of this resort were pristine, translucent, and sapphire. The most notable aspect of this place beside its paradisiac beauty was that a horde of green iguanas decorated the slopes of the crater among a throng of large-winged rare tropical butterflies.

Though quiet Edenesque, this place was far too tame and manicured for me…

CHAPTER 2

The *MISSIONARY DOCTOR of* PUERTO CABEZAS, Nicaragua

The Irishman knew I had made known to my mother by age six (allegedly), I wanted to grow up to become a SURGEON. And, as my knowledge of jungles increased, he knew I'd also considered becoming a missionary doctor.

From my early youth, by age six, I'd been aware my *"sailor-pharmacist"* Stepfather had desired to become a physician. I admired my Stepfather. I thought he'd love me with far greater depth were I to aspire to become what he himself had wanted to become. Knowing how sincere my intent was to please him, he'd often taken me to his pharmaceutical lab, and, given the intelligence I was purported to possess, he'd let me help with the surgeries necessary to determine what medicinal dose might be extrapolated from albino rats to affect human well-being. From this experience my notion to become a surgeon was encouraged.

Knowing this history of me, the Irishman thought it would be great to invite his daughter and me to hitch a flight with him and Parky on Parky's single engine **red** Cessna to Puerto Cabezas, the outpost of a missionary doctor. Parky had been asked to deliver medical supplies to the "*mission*."

The missionary doctor was the only man of medicine for miles around on the eastern half of Nicaragua! The flight would be a bit daring for we'd have to fly 250 miles over an unforgiving rapacious primordial botanical mat before reaching the doctor's clinic. Were trouble encountered, were the plane to fail, there'd be no place to land except over the top of hundred-foot trees or the surface of turbulent raging waters. Death would be certain. With appropriate apprehension, "*Jane*" and I; her father and Parky flew into the troposphere on a day stormy and wet…

Puerto Cabezas existed at the edge of the cascades of the coastal Caribbean side of Nicaragua. It was once referred to as the "*Mosquito Coast*." By legend, the "*Mosquito Coast*," during centuries past, had been purported to have been the haunt of **bloodthirsty**, scimitar welding "*Pirates*." In places where stealth abides, it was fabled, at least back in the 60's, there were hidden buried treasures of great wealth still to be found sequestered within the limestone caves of the coastline!

After several hours, we approached the Puerto Cabezas runway. Amidst the jungle, it was barely discernible. As bad as the Managua Airport had been, this runway was far worse ~ there were potholes, tree stumps, boulders, gauged out cart tracks, and forest overgrowth. Fortunately, Parky had landed there many times and knew how best to avoid destroying his plane…

BUT…

As we approached the *"landing"* strip near the *"village,"* the plane's landing gear failed to descend. Every attempt to *"drop the wheels"* failed. Closer and closer we came…yet there were no wheels with which to land! If we were forced to land on the plane's belly, given the missionary's runway ended at the edge of steep cliffs pounded far below by the ocean, it was certain our plane would have sheared over the cliffs and washed out to sea still loaded with the dead meat of our bodies to present as a feast for sharks!

As panic rose within me, I noticed neither the Irishman nor Parky seemed too threatened by our predicament. I soon discovered the reason. The World War II fighter pilot flipped a hood between he and Parky to reveal a **red** stick that kinda' looked like a tire jack. He began cranking it with great effort and urgency. The wheels began to descend until in position for landing.

A white guy, standing near the *"air strip"* had been watching the entire harrowing escapade. He was the missionary doctor. With jubilant excitement and a huge white toothed smile, the doctor nearly shook our hands off our arms when we greeted him! He said, *"Thank God, you made it!"*

At eighteen, without scrutinizing a person's inner soul, I was quick to judge them based on how they looked and what they wore but **NOT** on their character. In his late twenties (an old man by my standards) the missionary doctor was almost bald but still had a rim of long unruly curly black hair grown past the nape of his neck and out over his ears.

He wore gold-plated spectacles. Physically, he was a grunt with narrow shoulders, bony arms, and scrawny legs; big feet; delicate fingers (He reminded me of my pharmaceutical Stepfather.). He wore faded, torn surgical scrub tops and khaki shorts and dusty leather sandals. His features were somewhat paedomorphic in that his muscularity was more adolescent than manly. The only "*manly*" manifestation he bore was that he was VERY hairy ~ except for the bald crown of his head. He was short. He walked hunched over yet tilted his head back. This posture revealed an oversized Adam's apple and the appearance reminiscent of a tortoise! He walked rapidly, spoke rapidly, and had a Brooklyn accent. Though he must have been a man of great intelligence and possibly of noble character, the fact he was an effeminate nerd left me unimpressed.

I met his wife and two children ~ all redheads: all good looking. Despite my impression this guy was no lothario, the fact he'd impregnated a beautiful Scottish woman twice and she'd agreed to be immured at the edge of a remote jungle upset the equilibrium of my assumed notions of the things that attract women…?

The doctor took me to his clinic. It was a modest gabled thatched roof building. Wooden pylons carried the building four feet above the ground. Its walls had been constructed with local bamboo. The building sat near cliffs that plunged several hundred vertical feet onto an alcove of black sand. Exposed coral rock methodically was pummeled by massive Caribbean waves. Briny plumes sprayed through several cavernous blowhole geysers. Despite this vertiginous location, at least the entrance of the clinic was approached by a staircase of split log roughhewn wooden steps opposite the cliff so that, while within the building, you'd not realize how close you might have been to plunging over the side of the escarpment. Inside, two rows of white linen "*patient beds*" were present. One of the walls of this "*clinic*" was completely covered by a huge black "*communication*" device with many knobs and buttons and flickering lights (Today, that wall of "*computers*" could probably sit atop a single desk!).

While there, the doctor interrupted our banalities to speak through a stainless-steel antiquated microphone to a university in the U.S. about a patient for whom he was concerned. I then realized that the wall of "*knobs and lights*" helped "*the doc*" communicate with fellow physicians when necessary ~ from every continent of the world!

The family had habituated a Scarlet McCaw they called "*Beelzebub*" (bad bird; the devil). The parrot sat on its perch talking the entire time uninterrupted by our presence...

My fantasy impression of the life of a "*missionary doctor*," instilled by many "*jungle*" movies I'd watched, was dispelled by this visit. I knew, for me, being cloistered far off on a remote parchment of earth isolated from all else, condemned to help only a few in need of medical capabilities, capabilities severely restricted by resource and technology, was NOT for me. Though I respected the doctor's cause, missionary medicine was not as I'd dreamt. I reasoned I could be far more an asset to humanity by being a surgeon capable of helping many rather than a few. In a sense, this fortuitous, accidental encounter set my "*destiny*" in life on a different path. It was an "*inverse*" concatenation ~ a "*link*" removed from the chain...

That evening we flew back to Managua.

CHAPTER 3

ADVENTURES *at* MASACHAPE BEACH

It seemed there could be no great misfortune encountered upon the idyllic black sands of Masachape Beach . But this seascape was as deceivingly treacherous as the coil of a boa. Amazingly, within an elapse of time no greater than twenty-four hours, I'd experienced more danger and adventure than ever I could have dreamt…!

The **SCABROUS PASSAGE** *to the* **SEA**

My girlfriend's father had been asked to help a farmer of cotton rid his fields of *"black iguanas."* The farmer's field was near Masachape Beach…

The three of us, me, the pilot, and his daughter, my *"Jane,"* piled into his jeep and drove out of the southwestern part of Managua within the crisp twilight hours of dawn before the heat of day. We headed toward the Pacific black igneous sands of Masachape Beach. Clouds of steamy evaporate had begun to rise off the jungle floor; crystalline dew still bejeweled the flowers and leaves of the forest. The night had been burdened by thunderous cataracts of rain but, within the primal hours of this dawn, the sky had since become totally cloudless and pastel blue. We traveled a dirt road, muddy, slippery; guttered. The tranquility of our ride was plagued by cobbles of lava that rattled our jeep, shallow riverbeds that drenched our clothes and botanical overgrowth that held captive our progress. But, eventually, we arrived at Masachape Beach...

MASACHAPE BEACH

Despite a night of deluge, Masachape Beach was dry as a bone by the time we arrived. Its magma had been ground to a powdery dust upon which there appeared to have never been a drop of rain.

As we broke from the jungle onto the beach, the Irishman gunned the jeep's motor then slammed on the brake. This sent us spinning toward a circular clearing near a tall crescent of a black magma barchan whose "*horns*" dipped into the sea. A cloud of billowing reddish- black dust swept over the jeep. He then turned the jeep's ignition off and hopped out. As though he was a "*Musketeer*" bedecked with saber and plumed hat, he genuflected, looked up, and bid us, "*Have a great day.*" With that, he departed saying he had business with a local cotton farmer and that he'd return "*soon…*"

A bit worried and confused we'd been so readily abandoned, it took us a while before we, ourselves, finally hopped out of the jeep and surveyed our surroundings.

To the west of us was a vast pelagic sea ~ not the kind common to the Caribbean; not the kind harboring transparent azure waters made sapphire as their fathoms deepened past coral reefs. This sea was opaque ~ a wash of water between sapphire and indigo at its very onset. Behind us, to the east, rose a mountainous volcanic slope composed of black earth laden impenetrably by the malachite forest of the Masachape jungle. Along the coast, to either side of us, outcrops of weathered igneous rock stretched into the sea. It'd made unique the sea's bathymetry.

Where the jeep had come to rest, just outside the circular dirt clearing, there was an abandoned "*beach shack*" that sat several feet above the sand on wooden stilts. It had a veranda cloaked in dark shadow.

In addition to the "*beach shack*" there were a few curious incongruities near it. Although the "*palapa*" itself had no electricity, let alone a toilet or fresh water, there was a curious electric wire coursing out from the jungle onto a nearby rough-cut tall wooden lamp pole. The pole seemed to have a tin shade covering a functioning clear glass light bulb we assumed came lit as the day darkened. In addition, beneath the lamp pole sat an obsolete faded Coca cola machine whose metal still retained an enameled logo featuring a bubbling coke bottle and a sign that read: "*5 cents.*" The machine itself was half buried in a barchan of black sand.

I could see that the bizarre electric wire attached to the light pole also seemed attached to the coke machine. I thought, despite the coke machine stood isolated in this remote locale, since the electric wire seemed connected to it, there might be a possibility the machine was functional. I took a closer look. It had a vertical narrow slit window. Its window was *"frosted"* and cool to the touch. Wiping away the condensate, I could see displayed a row of vintage nine-inch glass bottles of Coca cola! Skeptical anything would come of it, but thirsty, I plopped in a nickel. The machine groaned. I heard a latch release. I retrieved a coke. It was cold! Slapping its lid off against a post, I brought it back to my *"woman."* We shared its content, left the bottle on the veranda of the hut, and then headed out to explore the beach.

The tide was low. Outcrops of basalt were exposed. They left crystalline glistening pools brimming with strange creatures ~ exotic seashells, spiny sea urchins, stinging gelatinous anemones, creeping starfish, spongy sea cucumbers, weird kaleidoscopic nudibranchs, and one octopus so slimy it could not be captured ~ it slipped through our hands and disappeared. During our exploration, we found a half-buried Mason glass jar. We used it to collect brightly colored abandoned seashells as we meandered along the shallows of the beach.

After a bit, our white skin had begun to feel the effects of noonday sun. We sought to enter the beach into deeper waters to get relief from the intense heat, but we decided it best to return to the shade of the *"shack."* The opaque tide gave an aura of wickedness that made it seem wiser to blister in the sun than to risk being mauled by some unseen sea creature. We'd heard unsettling stories about the beach before we'd arrived:

> The waters of Masachape Beach had a blood curdling
> history of death, decapitation, and deformity from the
> pernicious bite of its sharks. It was said, along the stretch
> of this beach, it was not uncommon to see aborigines

missing limbs or large segments of their body. Worse, of those that'd survived, it seemed the attack did NOT occur in the depths of the sea but within its shallows!

BLACK *"Spiny-Tailed"* CTENOSAURS

Past midday, the 6'4" fighter pilot returned carrying two 0.308 caliber Winchester rifles. He handed me one. He informed me the cotton farmer he'd visited, among other issues regarding crop dusting, had asked him if he didn't mind shooting a few black spiny-tailed ctenosaurs (**black iguanas**) that were destroying his cotton crop?

The Irishman agreed to help the farmer in this regard. He also thought it would be great *"sport"* and an adventure for me if I helped him. Although I was a carnivore, an eater of flesh, I had never come eye to eye with the things I ate while they lived. They were always presented in phlegmatic *"packages."* I don't think I could have then or even now, have looked a breathing animal in the eye and then killed it without remorse unless I was starving or unless I was being threatened by it or unless I found some humanitarian reason to end its life. But the *"black iguana"* had become a scourge to the farmer's well-being; they were destroying his cotton crop; his livelihood. The Irishman and I rationalized it a noble pursuit to help the farmer by reducing the *"infestation"* of ravenous black lizards.

Though hesitant, I agreed to help him kill the *"ravagers of cotton."* My amative damsel stayed behind beneath the veranda. I and the mighty warrior, her father, took off afoot to the farmer's cotton field.

Literally hundreds of black voracious reptiles beaded the fields of cotton ~ chewing and munching the farmer into poverty. We sat on a mound of dirt. The pilot loaded our rifles (I had never shot a real rifle) and dropped a large canister of ammo for reloading. Taking aim (I was good at that part), he and I must have shot close to a hundred before we tired of the event. Lizards were strewn dead and dying all over the field and yet, it seemed we had hardly made a dent in their abundance. The lizards were not removed. They were allowed to lie where they'd perished to serve as "*fertilizer.*"

The HUMILIATING CASE *of* SCYBALOUS

After our failed attempt at reptilian genocide, we returned to the shack where we'd left the fighter pilot's daughter ~ my one and only true love. She was not where we'd left her. Looking about, off in the far distance, we finally could see her strawberry-blonde hair bouncing in the breeze as she periodically bent down as though to pick up something. We deduced she'd wandered down the beach still looking for more seashells.

This was a great moment for me. I had had to defecate for hours. There had been no place yet to accommodate this urgent need. I hadn't found time to locate a "*secretive*" place where my anatomy couldn't be embarrassingly exposed, nor the product egressed to be scrutinized! So, despite the excruciating torment welling "*in waves*" within me, I'd managed to temporarily bear this burden...**ALL DAY**!

At eighteen, the thought of being spied upon while indulging in this natural obligatory phenomenon was an embarrassing, humiliating and unbearable thought. I'd have rather died than have been discovered "*compromised*" by the "*Irish lass*" that held my heart…

The fighter pilot came to my rescue. Empathy laid writ across his face and mannerisms. With absolute sympathy for my condition and my need to hide it from his daughter, the pilot pointed to another enclave far distant in the opposite direction from where his daughter had wandered. We agreed he'd not call her to the shack until I returned or, at least, not until I could not be discovered in unromantic form.

Faring not too well, I snuck off toward a distant enclosure the pilot had recommended. At first I saw only a black mound of pyroclastic rock long ago escaped from the sloping jungle into the ocean. Climbing to its peak, I was relieved to see it held a small enclave of black volcanic sand surrounded by a thirty-foot crescent wall perfect for privacy and my need. Scurrying down its sharp edges, I made it to the beach, dropped my drawers, and…waited. Nothing came as readily as I had expected. I'd held that which sat in my colon until all its water had been siphoned. Only rocks were left. I had developed scybalous (A scybalum is a hard ball of feces associated with failure to defecate in a timely fashion; scybala, the plural form, is released as a flow of hard pebbles.). With great effort, in a squat not far from the hot searing sand, I painfully gave effort to relieve me of this burden. Like a pile of sea turtle eggs, the "*pebbles*" were finally released. There, fortunately, was no need to wipe so dry was the expulsion.

Unexpectedly, I heard riotous giggles. Looking up, my face turned **tomato red**. To my utter humiliation, I suddenly realized a small flock of aborigine children had found their way to the top of the enclave and had witnessed my unedited condition. Off they ran, giggling, cajoling themselves about the *"gringo's poop."* Eventually, there was silence. Suffering a residue of embarrassment not quite quelled, I was once again alone tucked into the cup of the cove.

The SQUALL

As I'd gradually recovered my dignity from the event of scybalous, a strange atmospheric phenomenon had crept into the sky...

Within an instant, the beach had darkened. Surging clouds had insinuated themselves into what had once been a clear sky. Coolness slithered onto the beach. A blustery wind rose. It whipped the sand to bite my flesh. Where I stood, the beach began siphoning away as the tide surged forward and submerge the enclave of the barchan...

I backed away from the disappearing edge of the beach. I began to realize I'd be caught within a strange paradox. The sky appeared demonic at its center, but paradisial at its edge(?):

> Closing in rapidly from a distance, dark lumbering clouds rumbled as they erupted and bubbled and sputtered into billowing, undulating balloons burst to release torrents of rain that pummeled pits into the sand and came as an impenetrable opaqueness brought by the hand of God to punish all that existed beneath it. The bright of day turned charcoal. The warmth of the beach turned frigid. The sea, once sapphire and indigo,

turned stygian black and threatened with maniacal strength. Its waves rose to gargantuan amplitude and became capped white to release tornadic mists. The Earth began to shake as thunder soon brought spidery shafts of lightning convulsed into the torrent of the sea, the beach; the forest.

All this ~ terrifying! But at either edge of this beast, this squall, as sharply contrasted as though cut by a knife, the Earth appeared paradisial?:

I could see the slope of the jungle lit bright and Edenesque. Pastel pink and pale blue bleached the sky. The sun appeared as a haloed dot of cottontail white. Diaphanous hues of a variegated virga faded into a more distant cerulean atmosphere embroidered by rainbows. Stars not normally seen peeked through the indigo dark at either edge of the storm. The sea showed no rage. It appeared as watery glass tinged by chatoyant amber and light blue.

This atmospheric phenomenon had left me mesmerized. I'd forgotten the mortal danger of my circumstance.

The squall had advanced until it was fully upon me as an impenetrable sheet of rain. In addition, from the mountainous jungle slope, meteoric water had spilled as a raging cataract over the edge of the barchan. The beach had disappeared within the surge of this torrent to the point my body had become almost incontrovertibly submerged and trapped within its grasp! _

Purging myself from the entrapment that had enclosed me, I backed myself to the wall of the barchan's pyroclastic stone. I began to climb the edifice until I rose above the wash of the sea. Despite tornadic winds and the asphyxiating thrash of the deluge, I clung to the stone's cut knowing full well, were I to release from it, I'd disappear forever into the briny coffin at my back...

Just as the last fiber of my strength was about to succumb to its torment, as the Irishman had predicted, all such storms, here, in the Nicaraguan tropics, tend to abate abruptly..._

The spate of blinding rain whimpered into a foggy mist. The cataract off the wall of pyroclastic rock closed like a spigot. Only a thin drip persisted. The obnubilate gloom of the atmosphere, the clouds, the lightning, moved past the beach onto the crest of the jungle mountain and, like the slimy octopus we couldn't catch, it undulated ominously away toward the east past the volcanic slopes rising off the beach. The grumble of thunder simmered more distant. The sea ebbed away into eddies and tidal pools. Life came out of the sea onto the evaporating sand : *"beach hoppers," "roly polies"* (Isopods), beetles, hermit crabs, clams, blood worms ~ all scudded, hopped, crawled, or dug their way into the newly anointed intertidal water. The sky at the beach had turned amber; it of the jungle, sage and forest coral. A pungent, piquant smell of rain permeated the air. My exit emerged...

I headed back to the beach shack. I found my amorous *"mate"* and her father casually eating from a picnic basket. I joined them. I vowed never to forget this event ~ neither its danger nor its wonderment...

The **INCIDIOUS CURIOSITY** *of the* **TIDE**

The day had been replete with embarrassment, grave adventure, and novel experience. Hours had passed as though they were but seconds. Before we knew it, in silence, we'd found ourselves staring blithely at the scintillations of the setting sun ebbing into compass of the Masachape Sea as it surrendered to the indigo of night...

With the coming dark, the character of the beach and its surround changed. Fireflies rose to bring flickers of luminescence into the forest. Distant aboriginal huts came alight with the flames of crude oil torches. The shanty lamp near the coke machine, with an erratic hiss, lit to shed pale sallow light onto the machine and a bracelet of brightness around it. Bats came to dance around the lamp and eat the myriad bugs whose doom the light had brought. Crickets and tree frogs began to call out for their mates and howler monkeys let loose their roar. An occasional tropical bird also broke its silence in search of amative conquest...

Still sitting, looking out into this night, I marveled how the isolation of this beach at the mark of the equator magnified the band of stars that spanned its horizon...

We became BORED...

The Irishman suggested we take an open-air ride along the shoreline to uplift our mood. But he'd become besot with whiskey. Though he still could regale us with tales of *"buccaneer"* adventure, he was in no shape to *"take the wheel."* He asked me to drive the jeep. He chose to sit in the back seat; his daughter sat with me...

Off I went tracking the edge of the tidal flow. Though there were stars overhead, they shed little light. The beach and the sea were cave dark except within the narrow beam of the jeep's headlights. On either side of that beam, I could see nothing. And, although I had no true bearing, still, I drove on mutinous with irresponsibility…

We were laughing, we were joyous; the air was pure, refreshing; crisp…

Suddenly, we were jerked by a precipitous jolt that killed the jeep's engine and brought us into a dead standstill. Not yet concerned, we broke into riotous laughter. But soon, when I discovered we seemed incontrovertibly stuck, we began to worry. The fighter pilot and I got out of the jeep, lit a match, and inspected the tires. The right front tire had been trapped in a pyroclastic shallow water rivulet fed from the mountain. A jagged groove within the crevice had clamped onto the wheel like the jaws of a steel trap.

Now that we'd identified the problem, it didn't seem we were in real trouble. He and I came around to the front of the jeep, my girl-friend revved the car in reverse, and we pushed with all are might to release the tire. There came a metallic whine, a screech, the tires spun and burned, the jeep moved a bit but ultimately sank back into the stony pit that had bound it. After repeating that sequence several times and failing with each attempt we returned to sit in the jeep. As we sat there not one of us could craft a plan that'd get us out of this mess.

The jeep's headlights had been on the entire time we'd been stuck. If the battery failed our plight would be worse. We turned them off.

The dark came alive, it shrank around us. It brought irrepressible claustrophobic dread...

Since we'd become essentially blind, our remaining senses intensified. The lapping of water against the tires, for the first time, was distinct.

But then...that sound, the lapping of water, gradually became more faint and finally ceased...(?)...

I looked out toward the black of the sea. My eyes, having dilated to accommodate the aphotic night, could discern, barely, the tidal lapping at our tire had ceased because the tide itself had retracted. I could see no evidence the ocean was anywhere near our stranded jeep. The nearby stones of past volcanic flow lay strewn about. As I waited for the return of the tide, an evaporate rose that altered their piceous sheen to flat black.

Minutes passed...

There came a far off muted din. It crescendoed. The earth began to quake; the jeep began to rumble. From afar, a diaphanous silvery blue ribbon of luminescence approached. It advanced as though carried by the crest of a wave. It thinned. It flowed toward the jeep and struck the base of the tires to disperse into a thousand sparkles. The water rose with a flurry of eddies until it spilled past the floorboard of the jeep, crept up past our ankles and settled no higher than our knees. The cadmium bioluminescence fled past the jeep toward the distant aboriginal torches at the base of the volcanic mountain.

The water became quiescent. The tug against our bodies momentarily ceased. But then, it resumed to press us closer to the deep. As the water ebbed away, a briny vortex rose around the jeep's tire to shift its metal and steal the sand beneath its wheels. A stridulously echoic metallic groan came and with it, the jeep's steering wheel twisted. As if an extinct pelagic demon had risen from the ocean depths, the jeep was tugged further downward toward the slant of the sea.

We sat shivering with shoes, socks, and knees wet...

Within this interlude, I deduced I'd not driven parallel to the beach. Instead, I'd followed this freakish tidal flow into deeper waters as it sank back into the womb of the sea. I'd driven further from the beach and closer to the break of the coral reef. Beyond that reef, a hadopelagic trench dipped to depths the graveyard of sunken ships. The tide had not been the marker I'd thought. It'd been a deceptive lure to feed us to the fish!...

The Irishman, seeing my distress, though still besot, sat himself aright and, with slurred speech, he began a soliloquy:

> "Masachape Beach is no ordinary beach. At times most perverse, given an innate strangeness instilled by the character of its depths, the sea 'slips' far away into the belly of its origin. Minutes may pass before it returns to repeat this cyclic phenomenon. The sand is laid bare. It evaporates the wetness from the hides of the life hidden within it until the next wave returns...

> "We'll be Okay. It's not your fault you didn't realize you'd

driven deeper into the shallows. When the next wave hits we'll get a hint just how deep that last wave has pulled us..."

Since this ordeal had begun, I'd not tried to start our *"metallic sarcophagus,"* the jeep. I turned the ignition switch. Nothing. Not even the lights came on...! It became clear we'd not be driving out of this predicament...

As predicted, minutes had passed before the next wave struck. Again, chatoyant, coruscate cadmium luminescence mysteriously lit bright the edge of an advancing wave. Salty wetness soon plowed into the jeep. It soaked through to our waist without bothering to rise slowly as had occurred before. I saw my white tennis shoes, the shoes I'd removed from my soaked feet, rise and wash past the jeep.

Now submerged waist deep in the opacity of predatory waters off the shore of Masachape Beach, my fear intensified. The wave ebbed back.

Having been soaked to our waist by the slimy diatomaceous life brought by the second tidal flow, it had become forebodingly clear the jeep had been driven not just a bit further but had been driven significantly closer to the abysmal fathoms of the sea toward depths no light came.

The next wave might be the last we'd survive...

Though the jeep was not more than a clunk of rusted metal, it was the fiery Irishman's only vehicle; it was his *"beloved jeep."* He didn't want to lose it to the whims of the sea. To save his jeep, the Irishman knew the three of us were not capable of dragging it out of the ocean. He was familiar with the aboriginals of the native village at the foot of the jungle. He reasoned he could entice them to help him. All he need do is ask.

Because this night was far darker than most, he beseeched me to stay behind while he and his daughter sprinted toward the village for help. He believed, were all three of us to leave the jeep, it would have been impossible to relocate it ~ in the dark, in the expanse of the beach; in the reclusiveness where it had been dragged. He was certain he could return before the next wave struck, but, if not, he believed I could endure at least one more strike.

I sympathized with his plight. I agreed to his plan. He and his daughter left. I stayed. I would serve as a beacon of sound. I'd yell every minute or so. But, if no one came and it appeared another wave would drown me, everyone agreed it would be okay to abandon the jeep were that to happen...

Alone, I watched the pilot and his daughter vanish into the dark. Terrified but determine to demonstrate courage, I stood barefoot on the seat of the jeep and steadfastly grasped the front metal window frame. A cloud of *"steam"* rose off my body. I smelled like dead fish.

Despite my repulsive stench, a scent more overpowering affronted me. I smelled...VINEGAR...?

This new scent, this *"vinegar"* fetor, had gradually become more and more pungent. It'd become too strong to ignore. I'd been looking toward the distant aboriginal torches hoping to see the return of my companions, but the stench rising at my back caused me to turn to the glistening black of the empty seabed behind me.

There was movement...

Out of an accumbent mist came a tumult of dissonant "*clicks*" like that of a billion castanets. Enlarging pointillistic chalk white dots scraped across the waterless shallows. They approached. Their scent was as vile, as acrid as a bottle of spilt vinegar. It soon began apparent an infinite number of pale carnivorous **ghost crabs** had come to...eat me!

White articulated spidery legs approached the jeep and began to rout its metal. The jeep became awash with metallic staccato pings. A little bastard pinched my ankle, another clung upward along my pant leg. I could not help but imagine myself being rived to bone by these white "*piranhas...*"

But the clicking, the pinging; the movement suddenly stopped. The white demons seemed paralyzed...? After a moment, they scampered away from the jeep and back beneath their shiny pyroclastic rock cavities...

Ironically, it was another wave that saved me from the ghost crabs. It struck. It swept my feet from the jeep's seat and brought me parallel to it. I began to thrust wavering like a flag caught within a torrent wind. My grip held tight to the front window frame. Strengthened by fear, my grip had become indefatigable.

As the wave ebbed back, it pulled the jeep closer to the far distant reef. Eerily, as though the jeep harbored a phantom, the steering wheel, with no rational explanation, again twisted. The jeep once again lurched toward the pacific trench. I thought I'd met my doom but there came a loud clamor. A massive coral knob had caught the jeep before it'd come to the abyssal plunge that awaited.

In the black of night, still sunk to my neck in shark infested waters, and threatened by an *"incorporeal hallucinated wraith,"* I resolved, though scared beyond capacity, to NOT abandon the jeep. I trusted God had not meant me to die this night...

I heard voices...many voices. A throng of natives, the Irishmen; his daughter were rushing in the direction of my intermittent calling. It seemed they had been following the edge of the last wave as it receded. They carried a thick sisal rope. With alacrity, the rope was tied to the back fender of the jeep well before the next return of the tidal flow. As in a tug of war, we all yanked and pulled at the clunker in a line composed of a least two dozen men and one girl. Unrelentingly, we tugged. Slowly, the jeep was released from the coral and dragged into shallower waters. In the interim of *"saving"* the jeep, several times we had to abandon our posts to escape being taken ourselves as the sea returned. But eventually, into the wee hours of the night, the jeep was finally brought beneath the beach light near the beach shack.

The pilot spent the remaining night trying to *"purge"* the damage the seawater had imparted to his jeep. But no effort succeeded. The jeep was *"dead"*; its *"soul"* had been taken...!

The DANCE

While we sorrowfully stood still within the midst of the *"wake"* of the dead jeep, out from beyond the lamp's bracelet of light, came a curious old man, toothless, bent, wrinkled; one-eyed. He was burdened by a net he drug across the ground. The net held several rotting fish.

By the scent of it, the fish, the man, his fetid clothes, he must have been a vagrant living off the scraps brought by the sea. He shuffled past us heedlessly with jilted, spastic, asynchronous steps.

The World War II, six-foot four Irish fighter pilot spotted him. We'd brought a 60's transistor radio. The pilot turned it to a *"Doo-Wop"* Rockin' Roll number. He grabbed the cadaveric old geezer's stinky arm, spun him around and stood facing him. They squared off looking one into the other with deadpan expressions of challenge. The geezer dropped his net. It struck the ground with a dusty thud. Still staring one into the other they circled beneath the beam of light.

The pilot suddenly broke into a rhythmic high kickin' Irish *"jig"* without changing his deadpan expression. He then froze his last dance step with a leg bent off the ground to see if the octogenarian would follow. There was a moment of anticipation. The old feller began to dance. He and the pilot became wilder and wilder. They turned and twisted around one another; they flared their arms into dramatic poses and exaggerated postures. They howled and hooted; they barked and bayed as loud as their voices permitted. When the song ended, without one word passing between them, the old geezer picked up his stinky net-bag and wandered out of the light into the dissolution of the dark...

The hour of dawn was approaching. Too tired to find our way back to Managua, we decided we'd take a nap. All three of us sprawled out on the *"hut's"* veranda. Within seconds, we were fast asleep.

The **MONSTROUS** *"REPTILIAN"*

I must have slept so sound, I had not moved the moment my head touched the warped wood of the veranda, that is, the deck of this "*paleolithic*" hut! Every joint in my body had stiffened into the rigor of a corpse. As I roused from that afflicted state into wakefulness, I also discovered I could not open my eyes nor part my lips...

The residual salt of the brine evaporate from the sea and the dried tears of sleep had caked onto my lashes and sealed my eyelids shut. Cracking lose my stiffened joints, I managed to gently "*crumble*" the caked eyelid gruel enough I could part my lids. Bright noonday sun penetrated to where I lay and, at first, stung and blurred my eyesight. I squinted and rubbed my eyes into focus...

Attempting to open my lips brought pain. I discovered, just like my eyelids, my mouth had become sealed shut while I slept. During the previous day, I'd burned my lips. During my "*comatose mummification*" within the past few hours, saliva had seeped out my mouth and inspissated upon my lips. The two effects had "*mortared*" my lips sealed. Fumbling about, I found a dew laden coke bottle, wet my fingers with it, spread the wetness across my mouth, and gradually worked free my blistered and cracked lips.

Now that I could see again, I discovered my "*Jane*," and her father were nowhere in sight. But I was **NOT ALONE**! An ominous thing seemed to assess me "*judgmentally*" at the periphery of my sight. Fuzzily perceived, the thing that stared was far too close for comfort. I felt imperiled...

There, on the veranda, I slowly realized, a GIANT sauropodal "*di-nosaur*" was sprawled nearby within a ray of penetrating sunlight from a gap in the thatched roof above. The beast must not have found me threatening. It must have assumed me an innocuous rotting cadaver for it was only within the past few moments I had not thought of myself similarly. Otherwise, why else would such an impressive creature be bold enough to share the deck with me?

I turned ever so slightly to look at it directly. It was the largest **GIANT GREEN IGUANA** I'd ever seen ~ at least seven feet long! The beast's dewlap was an exaggerated masculine yellow-orange flag evolved for moments of salacious courtship. Its sub-tympanic shield was turquoise rimmed in sapphire. Its nuchal crest and caudal spines flared across its back as wanton cobalt-alizarin spikes like the spires of a cathedral. Its body cast variable shades of green that broke into black and green bands from the origin of its tail to its tip. It stared at me through a yellow eye with a black slit. I sensed the lizard's non-blinking stare was that of astute wisdom; the kind expressed when only one eyebrow is raised. I felt it was mulling over what my next move might be.

I shifted myself just a hair toward it hoping I might be able to capture it. The beast perked up. It rose. It rose on its front legs. Its inch-long talons clicked against the porches' roughhewn wood. Its yellow eye suddenly blinked followed by the erratic bobbing of its head. I knew this behavior was a thing for which lizards are evolved when they feel imminent danger or prepare for combat!

I plotted a capture. I wanted to show my "*woman*" the magnificence of this beast for I was certain she'd never seen anything like it. Fearful, but motivated, I leapt to where it lay. It was then I realized it had not grown so large by being stupid. It shot across the veranda, leapt six feet out onto the black sand, scampered with a horizontal spinous lizard-like vermiculate run, and ducked deep beneath a cavernous igneous rock. Though I searched for it I could not again see or find it...

I had been so excited to see the lizard I'd totally forgotten I'd awakened alone with no one in sight. Giving up on the lizard, I began to search for the pilot and his daughter. Just when I began to think I'd been abandoned for the sin of destroying the Irishman's jeep, they returned with another jeep borrowed from a friend.

The Irishman took note my demeanor of shame. He could see I'd felt great guilt I'd destroyed his jeep. With the charm and comfort a father might give, he assured me there was no need for shame nor any need for being forgiven. He empathetically expressed, *"I'd have gotten us into the same jam ~ probably worse!"*

We piled into the new jeep. Exhausted, filthy, worn out, and mindlessly silent, we returned back through the miles and miles of winding, *"eviscerate"* mud-rock roads until, late in the day, we'd reached the pilot's hacienda...

CHAPTER 4

Love Temporarily Uncoupled

The Masachape Beach "*incident*" had occurred during our second week in Nicaragua. My amative "*Jane*" could not, would not stay to the end of the month as we had initially planned. She had to "*prepare*" for her first year of college and, honestly, this adventure had been far too "*scary*" for her ~ she'd had "*enough*" of "*Central America.*"

    I, on the other hand, had fully intended to stay the entire month even though I too needed to "*prepare*" for college. But my allure to stay, even superseded my need to be with my strawberry blonde girlfriend! I felt I'd miss out on an opportunity of a lifetime if I left before the end of the month. Nicaragua was a place where the **GIANT BUGS** I'd read about lived! I'd already captured every "*interesting*" bug in America. Nicaragua presented an opportunity to capture the exotic, chimerical, mythopoeic phantasms found ONLY within the densities of its primordial forests; rare creatures that crawled beneath leaf and stone; that fluttered past flower and berry; BUGS bigger than they ought to be; terrifying, intimidating, creepy bugs; bugs that could envenomate, bite, or blister!

As the decision was being made for my *"Jane"* to leave and for me to stay, the World War II fighter pilot had not yet found, as he'd promised, an opportunity that'd allow me to enter the jungle for the sole purpose of collecting *"bugs."* It seemed it was NOT going to happen. Rather than be *"torn apart"* and suffering heartache when my *"Jane"* returned home, if I weren't going to have a *"walkabout"* collecting bugs, I decided I too would head back to America. It seemed fate had not wanted me to *"collect bugs!"*

Part IV

The **Search** *for* **GOLD**

CHAPTER 1

The "*PROPOSAL* "

Thinking my long desired hope to hunt bugs within a primordial jungle had been sabotaged by the uncertain vicissitudes of life, I fell into despair...

As is the primary characteristic of synchronicity, ideas that emerge as intangible thought, on occasion, become tangible reality...

The day before my departure from Nicaragua, an Amerindian, a "*treasure hunter*" of sorts, a short, stocky man of mixed-Mayan descent, had a proposition that required flight to a quaint, almost abandoned **GOLD** mining town buried in the midst of the barbarous Nicaraguan jungle halfway between Managua and Porte Cabezas. He claimed "*tons*" of GOLD still layered along the riverbanks of the Rio Bambana, a river that meandered near the town of Rosita. He needed transportation (a plane); he needed money to buy a sump ($500). Parky, the sixty-two year old with the single-engine red Cessna,, would provide the plane. The Irishman would provide the money. But the money would not be offered until the Irishman had a chance to "*dredge*" the river himself. If indeed GOLD was abundant, he'd give the Amerindian his fee and the three of them would then become partners.

The town of Rosita had become virtually abandoned except for a few miscreants and "*harlots.*" Its existence had been demitted to jungle encroachment. But it was rumored there was still considerable **GOLD** to be found along the Rio Bambana riverbanks at the edge of the town if hearty souls were willing to dredge for it.

The Irishman saw this event an opportunity to fulfill his promise he'd find a way for me to hunt bugs in Nicaragua. So, he offered me a chance to come with them to Rosita. I accepted! My "*Jane*" left; I stayed...

The ARGUMENT

At the crack of dawn, we arrived at the Managua Airport. Parky and the "*Mayan*" were already there waiting for us. The **red** Skylark Cessna had been prepared for the "*voyage.*" The Amerindian stood next to his sump. It weighed approximately 250lbs. Parky did a quick "*weight assessment.*" If the four of us loaded onto that plane with the sump in tow, he estimated we'd be about 160lbs **TOO HEAVY** for a "*safe*" flight...

A heated argument ensued between Parky, the Irishman, and the "*Mayan.*" I knew they were debating whether they should return me to the hacienda rather than take a chance on the plane not being capable of carrying the "*excess weight*" (me at 200lbs.). The heated squabble became more and more intense and as close to a physical scuffle as any three men can get ~ especially, the Irishman. He was the most dramatic; the most theatrical of all; the loudest; the one with the most flamboyant, flailing gestures. I sat on the tarmac certain I'd not be taken and certain the *"bug hunt"* was sure to become more of a pipe dream than reality...

It seems the World War II ginger-haired, *"alpha male,"* fighter pilot had finally convinced the other two if any problem arose because of the *"added weight"* (me), he would be more than qualified to handle it no matter the danger. With obvious reluctance they acquiesced. The three of them turned to look at me with expressions of exasperation; reluctance; incredulity. The Irishman turned to me and, with a nod, signaled for me to get on the plane, *"before we changed our minds."*

Parky, the owner, would pilot the plane while sitting in the left front seat of the cabin. But if there was trouble, the fighter pilot in the right front seat would take over. I would sit in the left rear seat and the *"Mayan"* would sit ON his sump machine. That would be the arrangement both to and from our destination...

CHAPTER 2

The "TOWN" of ROSITA

Out of Managua Airport, despite our weight, Parky managed to lift the plane's belly just barely above the field's perimeter of electric wires and overgrowth of capironata trees. We flew eastward above the jungle within the turbulence of a rainy season troposphere. Soon, there was only the steamy mat of a primordial jungle beneath us broken only by capriciously meandering rivers and the occasional ominous spire of an active volcano. Looking down out my cabin window I imagined how magnificent the life must be beneath my feet. And soon, I dreamt I'd be peregrinating within the thick of it. Intermittent torrents of rain trickled diagonally across my window. A flock of exotic birds flew past the plane from time to time. It was fantastic!

After a while, I noticed some excitement at the front of the cabin. Parky had spotted "*Rosita*" ~ a dot of grey in a sea of green...

As we neared the "*landing strip*," it was clear it had not been kept suitable for safe arrival. The field was gutted, potholed, sparsely graveled;

muddy. Huge trees arced intermittently over it. Although I was no expert, it seemed the *"runway"* was barely the width of the plane. As we came nearer the narrow impediment of the airstrip, intuitively, without spoken word, Parky released the plane to the fighter pilot Irishman. The Irish crop duster, with a nod inferring he knew Parky had not the skill to land this plane, took over and insinuated the aircraft toward the treacherous landing strip. He dropped out of the troposphere and flew barely above the jungle canopy. He lowered the plane's velocity to just above the cusp of its stall speed. As the field came nearer, he swerved and dipped and elevated that plane into patterns incomprehensibly difficult to avoid impaling us against giant limbs and tree trunks. I closed my eyes and awaited our doom…

The WORLD WAR II fighter pilot's aerodynamic skills were deeply ingrained. Somehow, he managed to fly safely onto a field I believe no other pilot could have managed!

The hatch was opened. We hopped out and stepped beyond the shadow of the plane into the steamy mud. The three of us rotated the plane 180° to prepare it for our planned departure the next day. We then began our onerous trek to the *"town."* The *"road"* was rutted by the wheels of antediluvian oxen carts and mired by the dung thereof. It glistened not with the reflective beauty of the sky but with putrid iridescent puddles encumbered by moss and algae and wiggly strange things. Despite the unpleasantness of the path, we tracked forward about a half mile before arriving at the edge of Rosita. The entire town consisted of a ramshackle *"saloon"* and a 19th century *"hotel"* and nothing more…

A bit parched from my fear of dying at eighteen, I suggested we three partake of the saloon first. Parky and the pilot agreed; the "*Mayan*" had other "*matters*" at the hotel. He departed...

The "*SALOON*"

Ferreting our way through the "*bog*" of the "*street*," we came to the saloon. It had been built from roughhewed wood stripped from the surrounding jungle. The wood had been weathered to grey but had become encrusted by the prismatic hues indigenous to the jungle. Lichen, moss, epiphytes, lianas, pitcher plants, bromeliads; orchids grew out from every crevice. Rusted iron hitching posts had been driven into the ground in front of its veranda probably to tether horses, mules, oxen, maybe even goats. Open window apertures without glass; partly cloaked by shabby torn curtains, straddled either side of the bar's baroque, nail-hinged, uneven, saloon shutters. A treacherous dilapidated wood staircase wound its way on the side of its structure to a second story that had two rooms for "*clients*." The front of the "*saloon*" had an intricately carved façade with faded indecipherable **red** letters that must once have indicated its name. We stepped into the place...

Past the saloon doors, the wood slat floor was caked with boot mud. But this was not the most disturbing thing. A serpentiform steaming pile of dog poop sat center stage. We dodged it and sauntered to the bar. Looking about, I noticed there were several patrons within the premises beside ourselves.

An evil looking, short, dirty, moustache-bearing, gold-toothed, un-shaven, greasy haired, flabby Caucasian wearing a sallow torn T-shirt and worn out grimy khaki pants sprawled out at a table off to the side. Unshod, his dirty scabrous feet were covered to the ankles with drying mud. He held a giggling, early adolescent village girl of obvious Mayan descent balanced on his lap. In one hand he held her bare developing bosom and, in the other, a bottle of near empty whisky. He smoked a robust but almost spent cigar. A machete dangled from his hip. He stared at us defiantly through the one eye through which he could still see. A jagged scar stretched through his opposite brow, disfigured his eyelids and cheek, and ended in a slight contracture the length of his neck. Paying heed to the obvious degenerate nature that must be his character; we did not more than glance at him indifferently; peripherally. Then, we went about our business as though he did not exist...

Directly in front of us we leaned against a rickety scroungy wooden bar. It bore no stools upon which to sit. Behind the bar *"repurposed"* Coca cola, whisky, bourbon, and vodka bottles rested on a shelf. Even from where I stood, I could see the *"corked"* bottles harbored unctuous fingerprints still unclean from the last patrons that must surely have de-spoiled them. I signaled for a Coke, Ken and Parky signaled for a swig of an alcoholic brew. A decent enough toothless white-haired, bent, ar-thritic, ulcerated, hoary native, took the cork out of the *"Coke bottle."* He handed the bottle to me. He then bit the cork off the liquor bottle and poured the liquor into shot glasses for the other two.

I don't know about Ken or Parky, but I scrutinized my bottle. Yes, at its bottom there rimmed an obvious living residue of some ungodly nest of creatures too small for the eye to differentiate. I looked at it hesitantly debating whether I should drink it. But I was parched. I rationalized, if I only drank it a bit and not all of it, I should be Okay ~ and that's what I did! I clenched my teeth hoping to "*strain*" any large toxic artifacts, drank boldly, spate anything clinging to my teeth and hoped the acid of my stomach would take care of the rest...

Bored, I pulled a "*balero*," a "*cup-and-ball*" toy from my pocket. I'd acquired it in Managua. I began testing my skill flipping the ball, attached by a string, into the cup...

There came a young girl, probably in her late teens, which proceeded to "*dangle*" herself provocatively, seductively against a corner of the saloon bar. After demurely staring at the three of us, she walked with a salacious sybaritic movement toward me...

"*You tink you want me, mister?,*" she moaned seductively.

The Irishman and Parky smiled sarcastically knowing full well I was not going to be capable of handling this girl. The Irishman finished his "*shot*," told Parky and me he was headed to find the "*Mayan*" to search for GOLD. Then, he left. Parky took a swig and slid closer to me as if to hear and see what might happen next...

As I looked at this ravenous unwashed beauty, she held me spellbound. I stopped playing with the "*balero*" and subconsciously stuck it back in my pocket. Like at rat with a hunk of forbidden cheese set in a trap, I hungered to seize the flesh of this resplendent aboriginal blossom of feminine allurement. She wore no bra. A brown areola poked half revealed with a turgid seductive nipple. The sweat and humidity of the jungle had made her thin garment translucent. She hid nothing. Large breasts, a tiny waist, full hips, athletic legs, even the dark of her pubic mound ~ they all beckoned. Her hair was thick and black and flowed with reckless abandonment past her waist. I tried not to look but for an eighteen-year-old, no effort kept me from staring.

Her hand to my chest, its femininity poignant, she looked up and repeated, *"You want me?"*

Looking down, I could see she may have been aboriginal, but her eyes were light blue. She must have been a mulatto of Caucasian-Mayan descent.

A primordial urge swept through my body to release the embarrassment of unwanted tumescence. She pressed into me allowing that which projected to be captured between her legs. I felt faint. My lips parted to receive hers.

Seeing the stupor her effect was producing, she smiled and let out a sigh as she elevated herself on her tiptoes, lips moist and parted, and squeezed even harder on that which she'd captured.

Shockingly there was but one tooth in her mouth ~ a yellow tooth with a decayed green margin. Her breath was that of a fetid sewer. I almost gagged. This affront saved me. I backed away.

My passion wilted. I came back to my senses ~ but just barely. With a discipline on the verge of abandonment, almost like the parasitized Coke I drank but knew better, I briefly considered holding my breath, carrying her up the rickety staircase to the rooms above

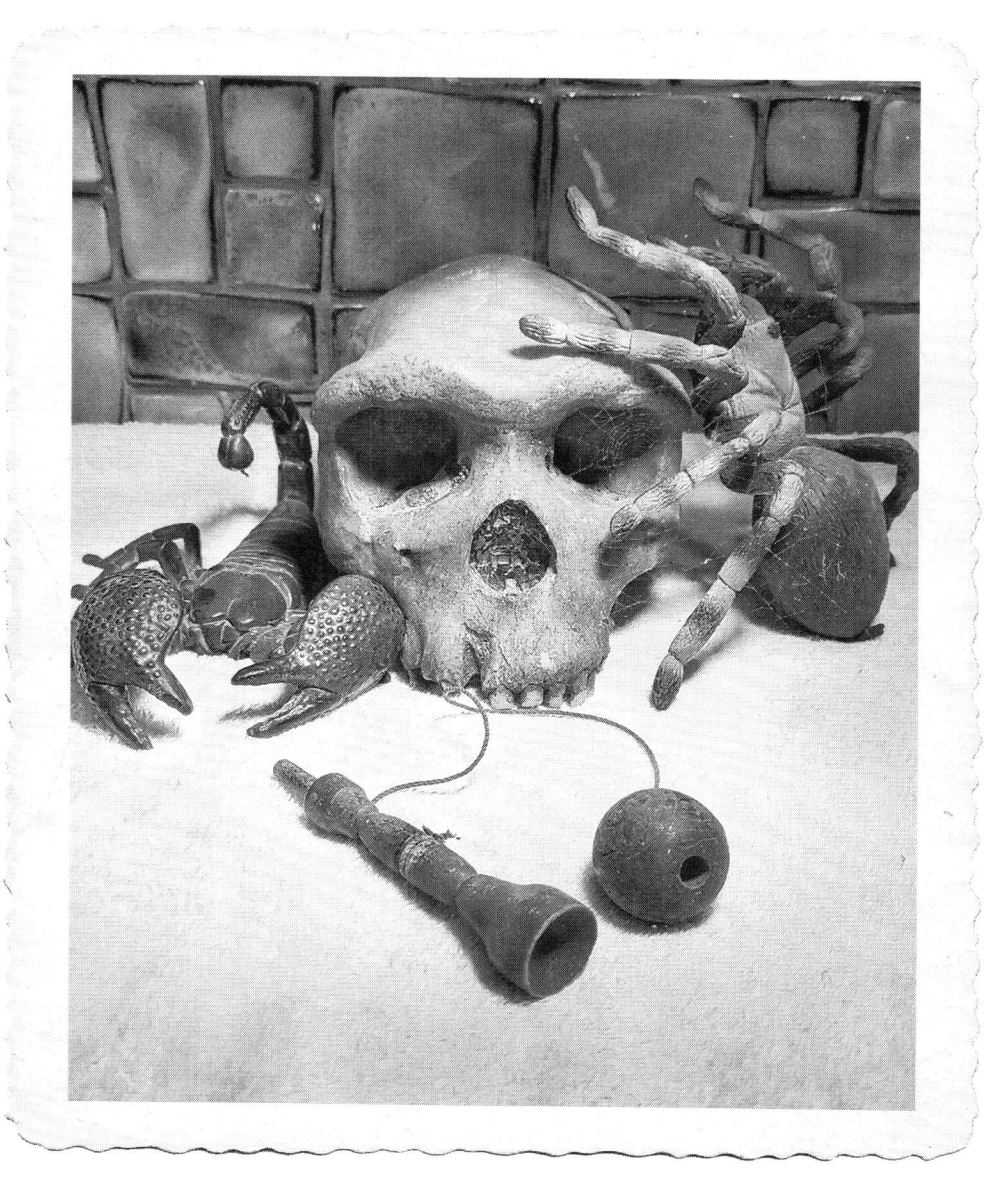

The "*ball & cup*" **toy**, the **balero** ~ still caked in mud from the jungle and swamp of Nicaragua, 1966

the saloon and dissipate the ache of my hormonal surge until she cried for "*mercy.*"

I denied her advance and awkwardly, in a near faint, stumbled out the saloon to find the Irishman. Parky, on the other hand, stayed. In fact, as I left, I saw that same girl narrow the distance between her and him. In mystery, the Irishman and I did not see the sixty-two-year-old Parky until the next morning…

I found the pilot not far from the saloon. He'd decided we'd sleep overnight at the "*hotel.*" Since the day was still young, he suggested I do a "*walkabout*" into the vast nearby jungle and hunt for bugs while he and the "*Mayan*" continued their pursuit of finding **GOLD** in the Rio Bambana at the margin of Rosita. We'd meet back at the hotel in in the late evening before dark…

The "WALKABOUT"

Its wood now oxidized to grey and decayed prematurely by the resurgence of jungle growth, the cavitous nihility of Rosita had been, once not long ago, cut free from the dense tendrils of a narrow jungle basin. And, within that basin, is where I began my trek…

Wrestling my way through a dew condensate beset by the coolness of the early morning, I'd come to stand in waist high emerald grass at the base of a long extinct volcano that rose relatively steep just past the "*hotel*" and the "*saloon.*" Before me, mercurial botanic novelty grew upward along the mountain into a cloudy mist that kept mysterious its summit…

Before taking the step that would bring me full into the thick of it, I pulled off my T-shirt and fashioned it into a "*backpack*." Within my improvised "*backpack*," I dropped a bottle of chloroform to asphyxiate the bugs captured, a box of triangular wax papers to store butterflies and a box of cotton balls to soak in chloroform at the appropriate moment. I then strapped several clear glass metal-lidded "*killing jars*" through the belt loops of my jeans with a thin vine. The jars would be used to capture the "*specimens*," asphyxiate them with chloroform soaked cotton balls and store them afterward in another container. Slinging the "*backpack*" diagonally across my chest I was finally prepared to capture bugs without my hands being burdened by these accoutrements.

Last, but not least, I'd brought one other item: a butterfly net. I'd use it if I encountered any interesting aerial "*marauders*" fluttering about within the forest canopy.

Although, in most "*jungle movies*" the adventurer is portrayed whacking through tangle and bush with a machete, I'd never needed such a thing to cut a path regardless the density of the Ozarkian forests for which I'd spent years becoming familiar. So, I reasoned I didn't need it regardless the density of the Nicaraguan jungle either. However, I did bring a machete to dispatch any carnassial beast or human misanthrope intent on doing me harm. I sheathed the machete and strapped it to an empty loop on my jeans...

Looking down at my feet I was ecstatic with anticipation. I knew, the very next step would transport me into a world I'd long ago dreamt about; a world I'd conjured from novels and movies; a world whose existence was unknown to me until my eyes beheld the movie "*Tarzan & His Mate*"...!

ONE MORE STEP and I'd soon meet the infinite creations of God...!

As I took that first step my foot fell upon fern and fungus and vine and tiny flowers and a mat of wondrous leaves ~ tiny mysteries of creation unfathomable, unrealized unless come upon by an observant eye. I knew I was walking into mystery and discovery...

Acacias, orchids, bromeliads, philodendrons, ferns, fungi, lichens, moss, monkey pod trees and kapok trees, cashew trees, mahogany and rosewood trees, palms, lianas, cecropias, pitcher plants; all engulfed me as I ascended the mountain.

There were exotic tree frogs, lizards, and viperous snakes. I only stopped to observe them for their unique beauty, but, otherwise, I avoided their capture. I even encountered a "*crab.*" I was befuddled.

I thought crabs were beasts that only lived in or near the sea. I did not, until that moment, know there were such creatures as "*land crabs!*" It was ivory with quagga stripes similar to the recently extinct species of African zebra. It challenged me with its stalked beaded eye, raised its chelipeds and clanged them like the crack of castanets. It was big. It was scary. I gave it a nervous poke with my butterfly net. It backed off and compressed itself until unseen beneath a fallen decaying tree trunk.

There were birds too: a "*two-note*" cobalt-turquoise iridescent quetzal, an "*owl-looking*" great potoo, a paradise jacamar; a mated pair of huge green wing macaws. I came to a tree I thought full of oranges until I discovered the oranges were NOT oranges at all. Instead, there perched a flock of alizarin cock-of-the-rock birds.

Upward I went until imbedded in a mist so thick I could see naught but a few feet in front of me. Though I should have felt utter fatigue by the steep slant of the volcanic slope and fear brought by the density of the fog, I was so euphoric and inspired my energy was endless and fear did not enter my mind…

I swept my butterfly net again and again through the grasses, the bushes; the thin limbs of trees to dislodge anything that may be camouflaged within. Weevils, stag beetles, rhino beetles, cicadas, carpet bugs, ground beetles, scarab beetles, click beetles, and "*jewel*" beetles fell into the net either from the swipe of a leaf or blades of grass or an outcrop of exotic flowers. Some bugs were not so spectacular; those I released. Others were so magnificent and rarely encountered, I kept and preserved them…

There were myriad butterflies too ~ some gigantic! I caught but a few. Most were too cleaver for me. With exacerbating frustration, I'd watch them fly too high or duck in and out of tangle so thick the net would snag within the botanic labyrinth as the butterfly, still free and wondrous, fluttered away into the inaccessible dappled light of the jungle.

Within this journey into entomological paradise, I began to realize "*butterfly collecting*" in a jungle was definitely **NOT** as portrayed in movies showing an "*effeminate*" male traipsing daintily through a landscaped flower garden with butterfly net in tow within the acreage of a mansion. Such a representation had ALWAYS irritated me for I knew

I was anything but effeminate and yet, I too collected butterflies. If anything, I fancied myself a *"priapic"* teenage masculine male!:

> In a jungle, the *"butterfly collector"* is focused **NOT** upon the ground through which his feet traverse; not upon the earth harboring slithering venomous snakes or hidden voracious predators! The butterfly collector's eyes see only the butterfly. In a jungle, butterfly collecting is anything but *"effeminate."* It's a dangerous, dauntless, fatiguing, exasperating sport enshrined by fearless bravery!

I'd trekked upward along a serpentine path for hours. The morning had faded into the late afternoon, and still, the mountain continued to rise into the mist. I felt I was so near its top I **MUST SEE** what lay beyond even if it meant risking being caught within the jungle's most predacious twilight hour and, possibly, even if it meant losing the path upon which I'd traveled were I to linger until the camouflage of dark...

Though the decision to continue upward until I reached the summit of the mountain was DANGEROUS and foolish, had I not made that decision to continue upward I'd have missed one of the most memorable experience of my life...!

The *"TENTACLED"* **ABOMINATION**

As I traveled higher and higher, I came upon the decay of a dead Kapok tree. Though such trees can reach a height past 200ft, this tree rose upward only twenty feet. It had been struck by lightning and was crowned by a multi-spiked trunk burned to cinder. Its bark had lost its tenacity and hung loose about the remnant trunk. I knew this presentation of botanical rot engendered an ideal habitat for "*bugs*." I prepared to rip a large chunk of bark from the tree...

Holding my open *"killing jar"* positioned for capture, I quickly tore free a segment of bark. This maneuver revealed a large, fleshy, russet *"spider-crab"*. The *"bug"* looked like an extraterrestrial abomination irreverently inbred between a spider and that of a crab!

The beastly thing had compressed itself into a sizeable planate ball. Luckily, the sudden exposure of this grotesque bug had not yet made it react. It remained as a stuck artifact; a giant swollen knuckle grappled grotesquely to the exposed tree trunk. I'd never before seen anything like it in all the years of browsing through books about *"jungle"* bugs. Its general appearance was repulsive. It looked fierce. I feared to disturb it for I had no idea its capabilities or nature.

I'd once learned that not knowing a bug could bring an unfavorable outcome and pain:

> Many years ago, I'd come upon a bug far more harmless looking than the bug that clung to the Kapok tree. I didn't know it then, but the bug I'd come upon in the Ozarkian forest was a *"wood spider."* That spider had a reputation that should have made any *"bug hunter"* wary. It'd been purported to leap several feet in the air, *"fang"* its victim with its giant pedipalps, inject a paralyzing venom, and cling relentlessly to the *"fool"* that'd tried to capture it.

Stupidly, I tried to capture the spider. I reached to grab it by its "*belly*." It leapt almost six feet into the air past my hand and "*fanged*" me in the neck. It clung to me so fiercely; no effort released it until I gave it a powerful slap! A large painful welt rose and took several weeks to resolve!

This thing upon which I stared was **FAR LARGER** than that "*wood spider*" and, like that "*wood spider*," I had no clue its capabilities!

My fear had made tremulous my hand. I'd held the "*killing jar*" suspended over the "*monster's*" body so long with indecision, the "*spider-crab*," like the legend of Medusa, had turned me to stone...

As all this "*pondering*" was goin on, a vulgar effluvium evaporated from the horror of the "*bugs*" derisive flesh. It was the scent of VINE-GAR(?) ~ the same scent exuded from the anthropophagic ghost crabs that'd crawled out from their cryptic pyroclastic enclaves at Masachape Beach. This fetor brought an increased amplitude to my worry what my happen were I to attempt to capture it and fail.

Fortunately, for me, despite standing over it for an ungodly amount of time, it had remained furled upon the bare wood of the Kapok tree. At the end of my "*measure*" to capture or abandon it, I decided I MUST capture and collect it ~ if for no other reason than it may be a species unknown to science. But I didn't want to go about this capture as stupid as I'd been with the "*wood spider*."

I decided I'd test its character by finding a LONG narrow branch so that I could "*nudge*" it from afar.

The push moved the "*monster*" slightly but, beyond that, it made no response. I "*nudged*" it again with a bit more force..

ITS RESPONSE WAS STARTLING!!!!

Like lightning, the "*spider-crab*" unfurled six scythe-like taloned articulated legs that sprawled outward into a ghastly dinnerplate diameter. Chitinous antenniform extensions sprang outward from its head and whipped past its body. Huge spiked, clasping pedipalp piercing arms gaped open to reveal powerful jaws. In a flash, the monstrous derision dashed askance beneath a residual enclosure of bark, compressed itself as do thigmotaxic cockroaches, and slowly withdrew a lingering hairy striped leg until nothing of it could be seen.

I was astounded; frightened. The event caught my breath, brought my heart to pounding, I broke into a sweat and trembled to the point I dropped my "*spider-stick*."

I now realized the aperture of the jar would not capture it unless I could think of a way to entice it to enter the jar of its "*own free will*.". I'd discovered it had run wickedly askance as it skirted across the tree trunk. I reasoned I might be capable of coaxing it with my "*spider-stick*" to the base of the tree trunk. And from there, I'd create an infundibular concavity camouflaged with leaves and dirt that'd track to the jar...

Now prepared, I lifted free the bark that hid the monster. With the encouragement of my lengthy twig, it grotesquely unfurled again into its full diameter, and, in saccadic sets of intermittent movement, it shot down the dead tree trunk hideously askance as I carefully nudged it toward the "*trap*." Its taloned appendages scratched and cut loose crumbling fibers from the tree creating a sparse blaze of dust. As expected, at the base of the tree, it shot beneath the thin layers of leaves I'd prepared. Reluctantly, it crawled forward beneath the leaves toward the jar as I coaxed it with my "*spider-twig*" until it reduced its diameter and crept fully within the jar. Immediately, I screwed down the lid of the glass jar, prepared a swab of cotton with chloroform, and asphyxiated it. Eight black eyes defiantly stared out from the glass as its legs folded inward into the posture of arachnoid death.

At the time I did not know what creature I'd captured. I thought it was a thing newly discovered by me. If so, my intent was to name it "*Arachnotarzanis tarzanii*."

Much later, fortunately before I'd made a complete fool of myself claiming I'd found a new bug, I eventually learned this "*spider-crab*" was a familiar beast within the same group to which spiders and crabs belong. It was a "*Whip Tailless Spider*" ~ an "*Amblypygid Arthropod.*" Despite its awful appearance and its repulsive vinegar smell, it carried no toxins and no harmful bite. But its giant clasping spiked pedipalps extending out from its head could, if a finger were caught, pierce the skin to **bleeding**.

I became aware I'd spent so much time trying to capture this "*extraterrestrial*," the day had grown far darker than when this adventure began. I realized sunset must surely be at the horizon, but the towering botanic canopy of the volcanic slopes and the thickness of the mist made spotting the sun's position not possible.

Within the Jungled canopy of Nicaragua
A PLANE CRASH 1966
& A peregrination into the ANTHROPOPHAGIC forest WILD... and then...
the ENCOUNTER!
There comes the Horrifying Tentacled ABOMINATION:
The GIANT "CRAB-SPIDER"
"Arachnotarzanus tarzanii"
Later discovered to be: the "Tailless Whip-Spider"
or
Euarthropoda phylum
Chelicerata subphylum
Arachnida class
Amblypygi order
Phrynidae family
Paraphrynus laevifrons

A "*Whip Spider*" collected many years after the original one encountered in 1966.

Having captured the *"greatest bug of my life,"* exhausted, drained of further *"bug hunt motivation,"* I decided to end the bug hunt and devote the remaining time to the pursuit of reaching the mountain top. I scrambled toward where I'd hoped to crest the mountain before total darkness enveloped me...

The **BASIN** *of* "*MESOZOIC*" **CREATION**

Finally, I'd breached the mist to find myself standing beneath a clear sky. The mountain pinnacle had torn free from the botanic morass below to expose a ridge of burnt umber and grey-blue limestone spikes lit bright by the last embers of a setting sun. This forewarned the silhouettes of its slopes would soon meld into the dark of night to conceal the route I'd taken to return. Yet, to see what lay past the ridge was too tempting. So, I struggled the last few feet of the ascent until I'd set foot upon a rocky outcrop overlooking what lay below.

Beyond the peak, the basin of a vast emerald-malachite valley festooned by floating mists, waterfalls, and capriciously meandering rivers stretched to the horizon. Fumarolic plumes of smoke lit deep by fiery magma rose out from volcanic calderas scattered throughout the landscape. The mating calls of all variety of creatures could be heard. The fireflies of the jungle, the *"click"* beetles, had begun to rise from the blades of grass, from the flowering stems; from the small twigs from which they'd clung during the bright of day. They began to light the shadows and the dark of the forest depths with brilliant streaks of bioluminescence.

Looking about, I was overwhelmed with the sensation I'd bridged a backward warp of time. I dreamt what lay below was a land of Mesozoic creation; still hidden upon the Earth; still not tainted by the stain of modernity...

So transfixed by such thoughts, I'd not paid attention to the change in the atmosphere. There came a flash. Its intensity bleached the colors of the "*Mesozoic basin*" and the firmament above briefly to a brightness that ablated everything to monochromatic white. Coruscate lightning then arborized over the jungle. Bellowing thunder shook the Earth.. In the distance, out of the east, approaching rapidly, there came undulating ashen-grey "*anvil*" clouds. I knew I was again about to be set upon by a blustery, tornadic, asphyxiating cataract of rain and wind.

As the storm neared, the last embers of daylight fell sharply away. Its tenebrous clouds ablated sight of the path I'd taken and threatened to wash me from the mountain. I prepared for the onslaught. Quickly, I tightened the bug bottle lids now loaded with bugs and secured better the vines I'd used to strap them to the loops of my jeans. The butterfly net would be a considerable hindrance. I dropped it at the ledge upon which I stood.. I disentangled my T-shirt "*backpack*," abandoned the stuff in it and put the shirt back on to help allay the nettles and thorns I knew I'd encounter on the way down.. I swiveled 180° from the "*Mesozoic Basin*" and began the descent I hoped would bring me back to the field of tall grass where I'd begun the "*walkabout*." Allowing gravity to give me compass toward the south, the direction I needed to head if I were to find Rosita, I headed straight down the mountain rather than take the serpiginous path I'd taken for the ascent.

Several times my foot caught an errant vine and brought me into a tumble until either I struck a tree trunk or catapulted into a sponge of vegetation. I fell headlong into several shallow sinkholes and once or twice I was caught within the narrow of a stony crevasse. But no serious damage befell me as I descended over, around and threw the labyrinth of botanical growth.

Lightning, thunder; torrential rain all came at once. Downward I sped into the obnubilate dark, into the yawning dusky chasm of this primeval forest. I had no idea if Rosita was beneath me or miles away...

Along my descent, the lugubrious phantoms that had whipped the Earth to unbearable wind and wetness, abated. The rain became drizzle, then stopped. The atmosphere lightened enough I began to see where to place my footing, but my sight was still severely circumscribed by the botanic terrain and the blinding mist now made thicker by the steam rising off the jungle floor.

As nettles bit my flesh; as pyroclastic outcrops abraded my skin; as projecting branches sliced thinly into my face, I stumbled, never stopping, awkwardly advancing downward; still relying on gravity to show me the way.

Eventually I broke from the jungle back into the freedom of the waist high grass through which I'd trekked at the beginning. Looking about nothing was familiar. I saw no hotel; no saloon. All that was recognized was a vast field of tall grass but no other marker upon which to rely. My only compensation was that I'd at least returned to a field of grass not dissimilar to the grass through which I'd first ventured, and I was certain I faced due south. Since Rosita itself was in the cup of the only valley for miles where tall grass had grown, I reasoned Rosita must be somewhere near. The problem was, I didn't know whether it was to the right or to the left of me? It mattered! If I turned toward the wrong direction, it could be fatal.

LOST

I was lost!

Fear welled. I prayed there'd be a "*sign*"; I prayed something might happen that'd "*point the way...*"

As I stood paralyzed by uncertainty, incapable of stepping to my right or to my left, there came another change in the atmosphere. It was though I'd entered a cave into darkness darker than the night. Not even my hand could I see...?

Lightning suddenly spat across the sky and detonated the ground in front of me like cannon burst. A misty drizzle returned and soon thickened into a deluge that kept me from breathing. I cupped my hand above my mouth so that the water would poor like a water spigot past my lips. The wind whipped into tornadic ferocity. It tugged at me and tried to rip me from my footing. I dug my feet into a thicket of gnarly bush and clung to its branches. I waited with dread for what may come next...

The Earth began to tremble with seismic groans that crescendoed until deafening. An avalanche of meteoric water, uprooting and displacing the jungle as it came, was descending. As the watery gauntlet struck the grassy field, it rose rapidly to my chest. Debris of uncertain nature flew past. I, somehow, did not lose my footing nor my grip...

The YELLOW **LIGHT**

As before, the storm settled abruptly, the torrent of rain ceased, the clouds, still besot by lightning and thunder, sluggishly ambled toward the southern sky. The stars and moon returned and, though I'd thought it gone, there appeared a hint of the sun signified by a thin ribbon of pale blue light at the western horizon.

Almost as fast as the spate had risen it dissipated. At first roiled and muddy and filled with things unknown, the *"riverous"* downpour rapidly distilled into crystalline transparency. The slender pea- green blades of tall grass once buried in opaqueness, came again into view. They feverishly undulated beneath the water. As the water drained away the grass no longer stood upright but lay accumbent crushed by its recent assault. A mere trickling of shallow rivulets bubbled and danced around my feet as the only evidence I'd withstood a thing that should have drown me.

I then noticed the blades of grass affected by the deluge now lay in a direction that I reasoned must have been toward the sump of the Rio Bambana ~ the river that ran alongside Rosita. **This was the "*sign*" for which I'd hoped.** The grass literally pointed the way. It was as though an omniscient universe had intervened to spare my life...once again! The storm had released a **synchronicity** for which I yet was too callow to recognize...

Now certain the direction I must travel to find Rosetta, a direction to the east along the cramp of the tall grass that abutted the ascent of the volcanic jungle, I paused to check my "*killing jar*" specimens before anything else. They still clung to my soaked jeans. None were lost…

Confident I no longer was lost but worried I may have wandered so far from the village it'd take hours before I spotted it, I sped my pace. It was not long before I spotted a feeble dot of **yellow** light smaller than that of a firefly but obviously lit by electricity. It emerged out from the grey mist at the edge of my vision. Concentrating on this light, knowing it MUST BE light filtering through the mists surrounding Rosita, I walk toward it. As I neared its glow, I realized it indeed was the light that emanated from the hotel I'd noticed when first I'd entered Rosita..

The HOTEL ROSITA

As I approached the hotel, I noticed a huge silhouette stood looking down from its porch. It was the rugged Irishman. He'd been considering entering the jungle to find me. When he saw my ridiculous upheaved condition, after recovering from a raucous laugh, he said simply, *"It's time to eat. Come on!"*

Before entering the hotel, I took a moment to scrutinize it…

The "*Hotel Rosita*" was a two-story structure. It had been built on tall pylons eight feet from the ground to avoid the consequence of the flooding rain and river. Like the saloon, the hotel had been built by roughhewn wood gathered from the surrounding jungle. Its paint was eroded and decayed. Vines entwined along its walls and crept into its cracks and crevices. Orchids, wild epiphytes, moss, and fungi painted its otherwise austere appearance. A wide wood rickety staircase led to the deck of its first floor. A second story balcony, enclosed by a balustrade, rose above this first deck and was supported by worn ornately carved wood columns rising to support it.

After ascending the unwieldy staircase, the Irishman and I walked into the hotel through a front door befit with the only aperture with glass in the entire town. It also was decked with an embroidered white linen curtain. There, we were greeted by a Scandinavian couple both bespeckled, old, grey, and bent. The old man shook our hands and returned to a lounge chair where he proceeded to smoke his pipe and read some tethered arcane book. His wife took the Irishman and me into her kitchen where she'd already prepared dinner. The kitchen had no air-conditioning; no fan; no refrigerator; no ice. We ate rice, beans, and potatoes beneath the light of a kerosene ceiling lamp against which the tall Irishman kept butting his head. We were then directed to the *"sleeping quarters."*

The *"sleeping quarters"* were on the second floor of the *"hotel."* They were accessed from the kitchen by climbing a wooden ladder to an open trapdoor on the kitchen ceiling. There, we were met by several reprobates of various origins hanging within the depressions of soiled hammocks. Some grunts were made but no one spoke legible words. Before sleeping, I sat near a candle to *"prepare"* the bugs I'd caught. I *"secured"* them in cigar boxes with *"insect pins."* Not knowing whether we slept with vile sociopaths prepared to kill us, neither myself nor the pilot slept without keeping at least *"one eye open…"*

Having failed at the *"one eye open"* routine, I awoke from a deep sleep shaken by a warm ray of sunlight that struck my face. I looked out through open arced doors of the *"sleeping quarters"* that led to the second story balcony. A gentle shower fell just enough to make the town, the grass, the jungle sparkle beneath rays of early dawn. It was so enchanting I detangled myself from the hammock and stepped out onto the balcony to allow the sun and the rain and the sight of this wondrous morning register irrefutably into memory…

The Irishman, a romantic to the depths of his soul, came to stand next to me. Enveloped by the jungle's pastoral beauty, the magical anachronism of the town that was Rosita, the pastel *"yellowish- green"* atmosphere brought by the misty rain, in silence, we allowed our senses to be saturated…

Our spell was abruptly broken by a yell of exasperation from below. Standing in pools of gooey mud, moss and *"parasitic wigglers"* was an obviously aggravated Parky. It seemed Parky's romantic sense had become barnacled by his age or perhaps it never was a part of his character. He saw only two ridiculous fools captured by the beauty of a morning he'd ignored. He was severely annoyed we had not yet prepared ourselves to return *"immediately"* to Managua…!

We hastily gathered our stuff and met Parky. The three of us plodded through the effluvial stench of the *"road"* out of Rosita and met the *"treasure hunter Mayan"* at the plane. We loaded into the **red** Cessna as before. Although Parky had feared landing the plane when we first arrived, he decided to pilot it on *"take off."* I packed my *"cigar box bug collection"* behind me in the open luggage rack.

Parky ignited the aircraft engines, the propellers spun into a blur, and the plane trembled and bounced over each twig and stone until its sarcophagus of aluminum skin rose upward into the air. We headed west once again within the troposphere toward Managua…

Soon, Rosita became a naked grey deforested patch embellished by the watery worm of the Rio Bambana. Toward a horizon festooned by a natant sea of mist laden valleys and towering volcanic mountains, we flew.

Reflectively enraptured and exhausted by the events of the past twenty four hours, wistfully, I leaned against the cabin window dredging into consciousness every second of my recent *"walkabout."* I was particularly excited about the bugs I'd captured and the mysterious *"spider-crab…"*

Part V

The **PLANE** *CRASH* !

CHAPTER 1

BLACK OIL

The plane took a mutinous bounce that dislodged me from my seating. I banged my head against the plane's side panel. The two men piloting the plane were engaged in a scrappy exchange. At first, all I noticed that could possibly account for their barbarous animation was that the sound of the plane's engine had become erratic. I realized something dire was happening!

The propeller had lost its torque. It had begun a dysrhythmic spin. Its "*blur*" had lessened to reveal the individuality of its blade just before it snapped abruptly into a vertical stop accompanied by the simultaneous resound of a pistol. An affront of black oil stretched like a splat of paint over the entire front windshield. The coagulum of oil was sucked and thinned to despoil the frame of the sarcophagus in which we flew...

The Cessna's engine ceased. There was only the sound of a fierce wind scraping along the plane's thin convulsing metal. The plane began a "*cadaveric*" descent toward the jungle below...

No longer capable of seeing either out the front windshield nor the side windows, Parky rolled down his side window and stuck his head into the raging wind. It battered this old, skinny coot so badly he couldn't keep his eyes open, and his legs were too short to manipulate the *"foot rudders."* As his head continued to be smacked and *"pleated"* by the wind, Parky tucked back into the cabin and, without a word, as though he could read the mind of the Irishman, he and the World War II fighter pilot switched seats..

The rugged Irishman stuck his head out the left window. Wind blew his hair into fiery flames of resistance and struck his cheeks so hard his skin rippled toward his ears. With clinched teeth glistening and rugged jaw jutted into the wind, he unwaveringly withstood the torment. The warrior swerved the plane to garner increased speed and airlift by taking advantage of the atmospheric currents and the favorable aeronautical physics war had nailed into his gray matter. He began guiding the plane into loops comparable to those of an albatross...

The heroic fighter pilot, by engrained *"instinct,"* managed to keep our plane afloat above its stall speed. Catching one current after another, the Irishman circumnavigated the air searching a place to land. But there was nothing. Below us and to the brim of the horizon only the entanglement of jungle, rivers, crags, and volcanic slopes encircled our plane. Our altitude was slipping. We'd soon be ganched onto the spikes of the jungle...

We needed a miracle...

"Look there!," the Irishman pointed, *"Do you see a yellow patch along the slope of that distant volcanic incline?"*

Parky responded, *"I do!"*

Far, far off, along a slant at the base of a volcanic slope, there appeared a flaxen blotch no larger than a postage stamp. It broke from the vast pellicle of jungle. To our daring pilot, it meant there might be a chance we'd survive after all...

Maneuvering with incredible skill, the pilot miraculously kept the plane spiraling toward the flaxen patch of earth. The once distant blotch of yellow burgeoned into an acre soon recognized as that of corn.

Unfavorably, were he to manage to land atop that field, he'd have to manage an upward slant of thirty degrees ~ a thing thought impossible! Worse, it became apparent the acre was pithed by decayed tree stumps. They rose as black harbingers of death. Within a matter of seconds we were either going to survive or die...or be irreparably maimed!

The Irishman set the plane on a direct path toward the flaxen patch hoping to reach it. Already, we'd dropped out of the troposphere so low, trees had become distinguishable and far too near. Directly in the path of our descent, two Kapok trees had grown at the foot of the field. We'd already neared the plane's stall speed (about sixty miles per hour). It'd be too dangerous to fly over them. We needed to pass *"through them."*

The pilot tilted the plane diagonally and cut through the two trees. Limbs burst free as their leaves ominously scrapped against the thin metal of the plane. We struck the field at an impossible thirty degree angle and glid over the cornstalks. By the *"Grace of God,"* somehow, we'd not struck any of the monstrous black tree stumps dispersed within the field.

The pilot broke the austerity of the moment. Turning to look at me, he sternly ordered, *"Dump the sump."* He knew if we were struck by one of those tree stumps it'd catapult the plane and throw the 250 sump careening through the cabin to kill us.

Without hesitation, I grabbed the sump and began to shove it toward the right cabin door as Parky opened it, but the Amerindian was still sitting on his sump. He refused to budge. He didn't understand why the *"pump"* needed to be jettisoned. Seeing he was **NOT** going to cooperate, knowing we had but a few seconds to get rid of the thing, I blocked his flailing protest, grabbed his shoulders, and lifted him so fiercely that his head crushed against the cabin ceiling. The Amerindian went limp. He was knocked out. From there, I literally tossed him behind me into the luggage bin where he laid amongst the bug collection unaware the predicament we still faced....

As we slashed our way precariously along the tops of cornstalks, I levered the 250-pound sump on the ledge of the hatch and released it.

Although the cornfield was a mere acre, its thirty degree slope and its cornstalks were a more fortunate blessing than we had anticipated. They served as a brake. Our speed decreased rapidly. At the end of the field was an impenetrable *"abatis,"* a wall barricade of botanic tangle.

Were we to strike it before our speed settled to a crawl, we'd be crushed like an empty tin can.

The plane abruptly came to a halt slightly more energetic than a crawl but slow enough it only rocked back and forth when it hit the end of the field. The plane had gently "*kissed*" the jungle wall so slightly not even the prop was affected.

Benumbed, I sat paralyzed, mouth open and drooling, as vacuous and as vacant as a corpse. For a metastable amount of time I'd been trapped at the thin edge of divine eternity ~ between life and death. And though it seemed the plane had come to a peaceful end; I truly was not certain I'd survived (?).

I experienced a dissociative out-of-body experience:

> I saw myself "*floating*" above the scene beneath me. Disembodied, the "*ghost*" of me witnessed the three of us and the "*Mayan*" sitting; frozen; immobile. We appeared waxy like mannequin replicas of our true selves. I imagined we four had died and that our fate would become a mystery never unraveled. My brain released a hallucinatory "*stop-action*" montage. I saw we four in stages of decomposition not natural; not over the normal time span but portrayed within minutes instead of years. I watched the horror of our dissolved identities through the eyes of hallucination as I witnessed the jungle twist and squeeze and strangle what was left of our plane and our bodies until we were lost to entropic dust...

During my interlude of *"insanity,"* the Amerindian awoke from the luggage bin. He was *"spittin'"* mad! I'd knocked him out so early during our disaster he was unaware the danger through which we'd just survived. All he knew was that his *"pump"* was missing. He began a rant expressing the injustice of destroying his machine. He yelled, screamed, and flailed about as though afflicted by a parasite gnawing through his brain.

At his wits end of tolerating the *"treasure hunter's"* exhibition, the Irishman turned from his cockpit seat and stared at the *"Mayan"* with a beastly countenance so clearly primal even I, though not the target, was terrified! Seeing the inflamed eyes and the threatening grimace of the Irishman's face, the *"Mayan"* abruptly becalmed himself!

I began to truly realize we'd survived a thing NOT survivable! I began to laugh. We ALL began to laugh. Our laughter became hysterical, raucous; strident. The plane began to laugh ~ it shimmied and rattled with us. The laughter regressed to occasional giggles, then stopped. But then one of us would begin again to chuckle. And, not long after, we'd all brake into uproarious *"knee-slappin,"* *"stomach-holdin"* rowdy laughter. This continued an inestimable amount of time. It was surviving the crash that made us laugh!

Though we should have been killed by dropping vertically out of the sky were the pilot incapable of maintaining a speed tenable for flight, or we should have been killed by attempting to land onto tree tops only to be ganched by the *"spikes"* of the forest or we should have been killed by catapulting into a bloody heap if we'd struck one of the field's black tree stumps or we should have been killed by being crushed at the far end of the field, all of these *"should have been killed"* events **DID NOT HAPPEN!** A sense of IMMORTALITY swept over me.

What was the likelihood, within a vast jungle of botanical growth that stretched from horizon to horizon, there'd be an acreage of corn, a patch risen upon the slope of a volcanic mountain? What pilot could have maintained an airspeed using only the aerodynamics of the atmosphere to keep us from dropping several hundred feet out of the sky? Who could have maneuvered a plane between giant trees onto a field slanted thirty degrees? How could it be within that very field not only did we miss every tree stump, but the cornstalks and the slope of that mountain were the very thing needed not to be crushed at the end of the field. How could ALL THESE things transpire to let us keep living if not for omniscient purpose?

IT WAS A MIRACLE...!

But our tribulations had just begun. We were in the depths of a carnassial jungle, long in tooth and toxic fang. We were inestimably isolated from civilization and standing on land totally unfamiliar. We might still die..

CHAPTER 2

The ESCAPE

Looking about, we knew we could not stay in the plane, and we knew, given the methods of communication in that day, it was improbable there'd be a rescue. We were in the cavernous pit of a vast jungle from which we'd have to use our wits to escape...

We fell to plundering whatever might be in the plane to help us escape. Sadly, I knew I could not carry the many cigar boxes full of bugs I'd collected. But I could NOT give up the *"spider-crab."* I found the beast, removed its *"display"* pin, and, forsaking my laborious attempt to deport it as it'd lived, sank, and secured it carefully into a repurposed *"killing"* jar. As before, I strapped the jar with a vine to my pants.

The fighter pilot retrieved his massive .44 Magnum pistol and stuck it in the holster dangling diagonally across his hip. He grabbed a sheathed machete and handed it to me *"for protection."* I strapped it diagonally across my chest. Parky had a machete and a .38 revolver he strapped to his hip. The *"Mayan,"* still pouting but silent, was given no weapon. We four than held *"counsel"* to decide how best to escape our predicament…

Since Parky felt he was too old and too enfeebled to trek from the jungle, he elected to stay behind and *"protect his ninety-thousand-dollar plane"* (I suppose that'd be cheap by today's standard.). The Amerindian wanted to stay behind hoping, if rescue came, they could retrieve his pump. The Irishman and I were designated to find rescue. We'd trek west until we'd either died from starvation or predation or found help. If help could not be found or if we died, Parky and the *"Mayan"* knew their fate could end miserably…

Unfortunately, we'd landed in the very abyss of the jungle. Civilization was not near. The Irishman estimated our escape from the jungle might take at least an eighty-mile trek *"as the crow flies,"* but he truly had no idea how far we'd have to trek. He warned we'd have to be wary of the aborigines that still lived isolated from humanity in the jungle. Some had been purported to practice cannibalism…

Since we'd landed in a *"cultured"* cornfield, it was logical there must be an inhabitant nearby with enough facility to plant the corn to help survive the harsh reality of a jungle most humans could not survive. The four of us found a path leading from the field that, about a half mile away, led to a thatched hut. There within was a pigmy-sized (less than 4'11") wizened old aborigine sporting a deeply wrinkled hide. His hair was grey and encrusted with mud; his eyes held the opaqueness of cataracts. Virtually naked, he huddled near a fire whose smoke rose to the apogee of the hut and exited a prepared chute. He spoke a barely decipherable tongue of

Spanish. But the Irishman knew enough about the native's language they could communicate.

After some argumentative wrangling, it was agreed between the native, the Irishman, Parky, and the "*Mayan*," that the native would help keep Parky and the "*Mayan*" alive until rescue came to save them ~ but, the native warned, there weren't "*guarantees!*" The Irishman and I were given "*directions*" from the "*pigmy*" where we should begin our quest if we were to encounter civilization. He pointed his arthritic, dirty, overgrown fingernail west and told us to stick to the path from his hut until we came to its end. When the path ended, he advised it best to continue in the same direction by following the sun and the stars. He indicated there were other small human "*gatherings*" we "*might*" encounter along the way.

We split. Parky and the "*Mayan*" stayed at the aborigine's hut. The Irishman and I strutted off at a relatively quick pace heading west. It was still forenoon…

CHAPTER 3

AFOOT *in the* JUNGLE

I was full of energy and hope at first. At eighteen, having survived a plane crash despite the presence of an impenetrable jungle canopy, made me feel indestructible. And, in the beginning, the footpath we followed cut through the jungle with little impediment. But, as the day dragged on, as sweat rolled off our bodies from the blistering heat; as torrential rains continued to slug us intermittently; as fatigue, hunger, and thirst incrementally increased and the trail became less distinct, I lost my initial certainty of survival. I hadn't consciously considered what 80 miles *"as the crow flies"* through a jungle of murderous beasts and deadly topographies might mean. *"As the crow flies"* certainly did NOT recount the *"true miles"* we must navigate afoot ~ the inestimable miles represented by meandering rivers, mountainous terrains, and endless botanical quagmires of the jungle…! I think, were the pilot not trying to protect me from utter despair, though he'd estimated our distance from civilization to be 80 miles, I began to believe he meant **1000 miles!**

The footpath eventually became uncertain; confusing; sometimes impassable by undergrowth. When the path was impassable, I did not pull out my machete to cut through it. That would not only have been stupid, but it would also have depleted considerable energy needed for our escape. We simply found a route near and continued to head *"west"* with guidance from the sun. And, if possible, we'd spot some directional mark like a tall capironata or kapok tree or the peak of a volcano to keep our track relatively straight. The machete was reserved for more dire purposes: defending ourselves from predators and anthropophagic humans!

Sunset came and with it, the guttural cry of the howler monkeys began, bats rose into the sky, and the mating calls of exotic birds amplified into a chorus. Click beetles, the giant *"fireflies"* of the jungle, joined this twilight ritual to emit their cadmium fluorescence. Crickets and cicadas sang.

The sun's last rays were eventually doused past the western horizon. Darkness crept deep. Stars eroded through the atmospheric veil. We knew there was but one star, if we could see it within the jungle canopy that would help keep our bearing west. As the sun set and night came, we spotted the constellation of the *"big dipper."* We followed the edge of its *"cup"* opposite its *"handle"* until we came to the faint handle-tip of the small dipper where we found **POLARIS**, the *"North Star."* Of all the stars Polaris varies little from its position. It doesn't follow the ecliptic like the moon, the planets, the sun, and many of the familiar constellations. As long as Polaris was off to the right of our shoulder, we knew the way west was straight ahead. Every chance given; we'd make certain not to lose sight of that star.

The forest eventually became hauntingly quiet save the occasional predatory growl...

Although the stars were more numerous and magnified than ever I had seen and the arc of the Milky Way an almost opaque dazzling white ribbon, such light barely shown down past the jungle canopy except as rare, dappled rays sporadically released here and there. Caught within the black of this first night there were many times the path could not be followed directly. In fact, the path we'd initially followed had long ago ended. So, we did what any adventurer must do, we created our own path. We knew, since the night was extremely dark, it may have been a bit smarter to stop our journey and maybe sleep until the sun rose out of the east to lessen the risk we'd lose our bearing, but our need to continue was urgent! The Irishman's friend and the *"Mayan"* depended on our escape to bring them rescue. So, we walked on...

As the hours came and went, I began to learn a few things about jungles I'd never read.:

I thought jungles were HOT day and night!
Though the day had been sweltering and had decanted the water from our veins enough to drench our clothes, the night had become unexpectedly COLD ~ shivering cold; goosebump cold! Our clothes were not only soaked from sweat but also from intermittent storms. We were losing thirty times more body heat than if our clothes had been dry. We might as well have been caught within a glacial crevasse at the North Pole!

I thought fruit and vegetables would be abundant! But there were none to eat! Sure, I'd read about all the fruits and vegetables grown out from the feracious soil of jungle terrain. But those accounts must have been filmed and written within the domain of **JUNGLE FARMS** and NOT that of an actual pristine jungle. The only thing eatable along the path were tree stems and leaves.

I thought MEAT would be abundant! But, as hunger gnawed its way into my brain, I'd never considered meat in the jungle did not come wrapped in phlegmatic packages! I hadn't realized, to get meat, you'd have to slay an animal yourself, gut it, and cook it or eat it raw if fire could not be started.

Though I'm not a hunter of flesh and prefer meat whose eyes do not pitifully stare, I'd kill a furry or scaled beast for food. BUT, we hadn't seen a single mammal; not a single reptile. They'd remained hidden and too well adapted to be encountered...

I felt BETRAYED! I felt some author of some jungle book, or some producer of some jungle movie should have warned the *"virgin"* adventurer about these things...

Now freezing to death, wet, shivering; hungry, I began to think about **FIRE** ~ for warmth; to fend off predators; to singe mosquitos. I considered I'd light a match. But we didn't have a match and, of course, were we to *"make a fire"* it'd increase the time required to escape the jungle.

I fell back into my stupor of increasing despair and lugged along focused on putting one foot in front of the other without slipping or stubbing my toe or getting stuck beneath a wayward root...

Thankfully, the one aspect of survival that we did not fret was access to **WATER** ~ it was abundant. But the only water "*safe*" to drink was meteoric water caught as it fell first from the sky. The water from puddles and streams and waterfalls and even water sipped off leaves was potentially lethal. Within the jungle, there were and still are a "*billion*" parasitic unseen bugs just waiting within the wet to eat you from the inside until they spill from your decayed body. BUT, since sixty percent of a human body IS WATER, if no water is imbibed within 3 to 4 days the body **DIES**! (More likely it takes fewer days than the 3 or 4 quoted given the diffuse sweating that jungles decant from the flesh.). Given that physiologic fact, we'd decided at the onset, infected or not, we'd drink whatever water came our way. Caloric food, on the other hand, we knew we could abstain for about 3 weeks.

On and on we walked. Through the night we walked. The moon arced above us and eventually began its descent to the western horizon. From the east, the bluish tinge of dawn diffused into the dark of night...

Dawn came effected by the translucent gloom of a heavy low-lying mist. As the sun rose higher and the jungle came into brighter light, amazingly, we found ourselves at the edge of a well hoofed trail. It led west. We knew this because the sun had risen directly behind our back. We knew such a trail portended the probability of another settlement of "*autochthons.*"

Before noon, in the distance, a thin stack of smoke could be seen rising out of the jungle. We quickened our pace along the *"ungulate"* trail hoping to arrive where further help could be garnered. The trail headed directly into a clearing of several thatched native huts…

CHAPTER 4

The "TRIBAL GATHERING"

As we came to the edge of a clearing in the midst of which were several thatched-bamboo huts, a cachectic, white-haired, wrinkled, bent, tribal primitive, bearing an attitude of authority, followed by three of his younger cohorts, advanced toward us. The "*leader*" was threatening. He advanced rapidly while brandishing a machete in a malevolent manner and jabbing his "*paleolithic*" spear as though he intended to pierce us! The three younger men tagging behind him, were a bit less aggressive, but bore scowling faces as they clasped their machetes as though prepared to use them. Though their attitude was unfriendly and aggressive, they could not disguise their fear of our presence...

The Irishman simply dropped his hand onto the sheath of his .44 magnum and indifferently met the native's attitude with his own. Mimicking the fighter pilot, I too placed my hand formidably on the sheath of my machete. It was clear to the "*paleoliths*," neither the pilot nor I were intimidated by them. Standing upright, both of us were of mesomorphic build, towered well above the parasitized men by at least a foot and we each outweighed them by more than a hundred pounds. In that our survival was paramount if we were to save our two desperate cohorts, we truly were prepared to slay the lot of them if need be.

Muscles tense, staring one into the other, no one moved…

Finally, the *"chief"* cracked a decayed, almost toothless grin, fell into an attitude of repose, and waved us into his camp. Cautiously, we joined them…

The Irishman explained our predicament in a dialect of Spanish the *"chief"* understood. He pulled out a three-inch wad of Nicaraguan money (for which they somehow were familiar) and bartered with the men until they agreed upon a price they felt reasonable for his demands.

From this exchange, the natives had agreed to let us use one of their burrows to ride. The donkey's height was short, too short! But, if we allowed our feet and ankles to drag along the terrain while we sat on the donkey's back, it would lessen the burden of our journey. Looking at the pitiful malnourished beast, we knew it couldn't carry the two of us simultaneously. We decided we'd take turns *"riding it."* Since the Irishman was a *"giant"* compared to me, we decided it best for me to ride along upward slants of the forest floor while he'd ride downward.

As part of the *"bargain,"* the *"strongest"* of the younger natives would guide us to a distant **SWAMP**. We'd have to *"foot it"* alone beyond that point. The donkey and the guide would venture no further. From there, we'd be left to forage through the swamp if we were to find salvation.

As a token of their good will, they invited us to eat with them. We were starving. We accepted. They brought us into a thatched hut with a central wood fire. A metal pot hung above it. From the pot, a matron scooped a mucilaginous *"clump"* of yellow-whitish stuff onto a *"plate"* of bark.

A *"SUMPTUOUS"* MEAL

Although I'm extremely finicky when it comes to food, I decided I MUST eat the stuff. Not only had I been well into the *"last"* stage of starvation, but I'd also felt compelled to eat it despite its regurgitative scent. I didn't want to insult the tribe. Looking into the stuff, I checked for wormy crawly things. There were none. But the stuff had an awful lot of black specks I knew weren't pepper!

Looking at me with a sly grin, realizing I was about to puke, the Irishman scooped a full hand of the gruel and plopped it in his mouth. With exaggerated gesticulation, he chewed and squeezed and strained the stuff through his teeth. Then he gargled and swallowed it. He smacked his lips a few times and then let out a sigh. His breath was awful! He looked at me as though to say, *"Your turn."*

Fearing the worst, I scooped up the stuff myself and plopped in a whole mouthful. I swallowed the gruel a quickly as I could hoping whatever it might have been would slip past my tastebuds before my tongue had a chance to register what foul thing was on the way to my stomach! My tastebuds and brain betrayed me. The viscid and stinky repugnancy of the slime I'd tried to swallow was too sticky to simply pass through.

A residue of it stuck to my teeth, to my tongue, and to my cheeks. It even stuck to the back of my throat. It was salty; bitter; unctuous; there were chunks of stuff in it unfamiliar. I tried not to ruminate upon it, the stuff I'd swallowed, but I couldn't ignore it!... **I was going to PUKE!**

Trying to stave off the insult that would affront the natives were I to vomit in their hut, I grabbed a *"bamboo cup"* of reddish-brown liquid to *"rinse"* my mouth and gullet. The pilot leaned away from me as I did this with an expression of incredulity and quietly muttered, *"NO..."*

He was too late. As the liquid poured into my mouth I smelled not water but *"burnt plastic."* I gargled the *"brew"* to shake loose the gooey gelatin from my mouth and swallowed everything. To my pleasure, that grimy, greasy, mucid film came away leaving my mouth once again more or less watery.

Within literally seconds, my vision blurred, my nausea became overwhelming, and I vomited not outwardly but into my mouth. Not to offend, I swallowed the regurgitant. Temporarily, my symptoms improved...

Fortunately, it was time to leave this tribal gathering. As the fighter pilot prepared to trek on and the young native guide readied the donkey, I snuck off to a tree. I puked everything I'd consumed. The pilot and the guide had already started up the path before I caught up with them.

As was typical within the mannerisms of this World War II heroic character, he turned to me with a bedeviled grin, stopped walking, shook his head as if to suggest disbelief and said, "*You drank the native's 'psycho' brew meant to awaken the sprits of the jungle. You're gonna' be a bit 'dizzy' for a couple hours. Lucky you vomited most of it..."* Then, staring at me quiz-zically, wondering if what he said sunk in, he turned away and continued onward. I was too worn out and hungry to respond and, in fact, if the stuff killed me it'd be okay. I couldn't have been more miserable!

Later the pilot told me he thought I'd drank ayahuasca (*"eye-ah-WAHska"*). It is a chemical that produces a hallucinogen that lasts about four hours...

CHAPTER 5

The PERILOUS TREK

Just past noon, we'd resumed our journey ~ me, the pilot, and the young native…and…the burro. At first, the path was a clear cut trail most likely made by the tribe and the indigenous mammalian life of Nicaragua.

We thought to spare the donkey until we absolutely needed him. So, the donkey tagged along while we continued to walk. The patriarch of the *"village"* had estimated, if we continued steadfastly, we'd probably reach the **SWAMP** within two days.

En route, the Irishman pulled me aside as our *"guide"* continued onward. He warned:

> *"I did somethin' stupid back at the native encampment. I was a bit worn-out. I wasn't usin' all 'my marbles.' To pay the chief, I'd reached into my pocket where, fortunately, in times of need such as these, I keep a three-inch rolled wad of money. Dur-*

ing the barter, the chief had exacted the amount he wanted me to pay him...BUT...he didn't know how much money I had! I saw his eyes widen in a way one could say was 'greedy' when he saw the wad. But our wager had been made and he honored his bargain."

The Irishman, after having made certain our native guide had advanced well out of earshot, continued:

"The primitives now know I carry a great deal of money. If we sleep, our guide or our potential assassins' from the village may ambush us. But they just don't kill ya', some cut off their victims head and...or...eat their bodies. Taking our money, our weapons, and our clothes might be just an added 'pay-off ' for them! We can't sleep until we cross that swamp and rid ourselves of this danger from the villagers or our guide..."

"GREAT," I sarcastically mumbled...

Already, neither of us had slept since the plane crash. Now, not only would I be starving, fatigued, and thirsty, I'd also not be SLEEPING either. I supposed it could have been worse. I might later have my head stuck on a stake or my body boiling in a pot! It seemed an impossible nightmare...

Although the new trail had not vanished into a thicket of botanic tangle as had been the case before, its terrain had become far more severe. All day we'd been forced to walk through crag or crevice, we'd been forced to scale upward and downward along volcanic slopes, and we'd been forced to wade through streams and shallow rivers aflush with boulders and unseen torments. We hardly talked as we walked except to signal a warning of trouble along the path. It was too exhausting to talk.

We'd twisted our ankles and stubbed our toes a thousand times. The young aboriginal *"guide"* had sliced the bottom of his foot along the way, yet, though his foot trickled **blood** through most of the journey that day, it didn't slow his pace and he didn't reveal the pain it must have caused.

In fairness, we would not have been so clumsy. But the whole while we walked westward (more or less) we had to search ahead without following our immediate footpath to affirm whether or not a deadly snake sat coiled basking anywhere within the dappled light of the trail. The pilot had warned this snake is so well camouflaged it may not be seen until stepped upon and the pain of its venom is felt! He called this pit viper the *"3-step-snake."* He said if we were bit, within *"3 steps"* we'd be dead. I later learned, although his account of the snake was a bit dramatic, it wasn't too far off the mark:

> The snake for which he'd spoke was called **Bothrop's asp**er or the **fer- de-lance** or the **jararaca pit viper**. The snake was said to be capable of ejecting its venom 6 feet into the air! I suppose were its venom to reach a mucous membranes of the mouth or the nose or the conjunctiva of the eye, it could be dangerous. But, if the snake managed to inject its venom beneath the flesh, since its venom carries deadly toxic proteins, death is imminent without access to anti-venom. Hemorrhagic

shock from bleeding from every orifice including the gums, the nose, the eyes, the internal organs, and the brain can occur. Death follows not long after these symptoms emerge.

If the bite is survived, it isn't over. The flesh at the site of the envenomation can rot through to the bone and may cause amputation. If the snake is decapitated, it's still dangerous! Reflexively, its jaw, even after its head has been severed, can still clamp its fangs into flesh and envenomate! It is best the head is left alone until it is long dead. It's a snake notorious for death and mutilation.

At some point, as twilight approached on this second leg of our escape, the fighter pilot dropped back to where I'd plodded forward and again came along side me. He'd begun to realize our fate might be less than fortunate. Knowing I'd never before been in such dire circumstances, he felt it best to impart his wisdom before things got so bad neither of us could think rationally. With a voice spoken through blistered and burnt lips, the Irishman's tone was most genuine and deliberate. He wearily spoke:

> "If either of us can't 'make it,' if you or I can't continue on, the one still capable should leave the other behind without waiting for the other to recover. If one of us dies, the other MUST NOT STOP to bury the body. One of us MUST SURVIVE if my friend and the "Mayan" have any chance to live."

I agreed…

CHAPTER 6

The **DEADLY** *"Strangler Fig Tree!"*

Late into the night we came to the pinnacle of a hilly outcrop flanked by boulders and several tall trees, one of which was a giant strangler fig tree whose configuration made a hollow worthy of shelter. Although our plan had been NOT TO SLEEP while we were guided by this native, we couldn't hold out. At that point of our journey, our eyes had not been closed for well over fifty hours. Exhausted, aching, hungry, wet from intermittent thunderous storms, eyes burning, and a brain no longer functional, we decided, even if our heads were cut off and we were ransacked and eaten by our *"Cro-Magnon"* guide or his family, there **MUST BE** a way to sleep.

The strangler fig tree offered an almost dry shelter, protection from predators, and a quiet place for a nap. Warily, we decided we'd trade taking a few *"quick naps."* At least one of us would then be awake enough to fend off the native or a predator if need be. We worked our way into the tree's gnarly hollow, brushed aside the deciduous debris ~ twigs, leaves, stones. We checked for a fur-de-lance, a scorpion, a centipede, or a wayward venomous spider. Having assured the enclosure bore no detriments to our health, we settled against the back wall of the strangler's *"weblike"* upward arborization. I offered to *"keep watch"* first while the pilot and our aborigine slept…

As I watched my confidant fall steadfast into a snoring sleep, my eyelids fell. I shook myself until I came awake. My eyelid's fell again and…I was gone! No one, as we'd sworn to do, was watching the native or the jungle…

I was STARTLED awake!

Having slept for an indeterminant amount of time after not having slept for days left my brain like *"cracked cement"* ~ no longer completely intact. When I first roused, I was disoriented. My vision was still blurred but I could see the pilot wildly animated and, unbecoming to his character, flailing about with bloodcurdling screams. I first assumed the pilot was being slaughtered by the aborigine. But I soon became aware the native was not involved. As I assimilated the event within the dendrites of my weary brain, the Irishman dashed from the enclosure of our strangler tree hooting and howling like a banshee. He was convulsively slapping himself EVERYWHERE. I thought he'd gone crazy or, perhaps, something had occurred for which I was not yet aware.

Seeing this romantic adventurous giant of masculinity behaving like a wimp, at first, was ridiculously funny. I began to laugh. But then, even in the dark of night what starlight lit his face suggested he was in true AGONY!

I asked, *"Have you been bit…or…stabbed?"*

Without composure, he gasped, *"I sat in a nest of ants! They're killin' me! Knock 'em off!"*

It was then I noticed his body appeared blurry; fuzzy. His clothes were undulating with countless ripples. Large black six-legged beasts skirted every inch of his body. *"Saber-toothed"* **BULLIT ANTS** were attacking him…!

I still had not completely shrugged off my stuporous state. I unsheathed my machete and started to swing it with the slicing edge directed toward him. I'd intended to crush the bugs by slapping them with my machete. It's just that it hadn't occurred to me the sharp end of the blade was not the end to use!

The pilot saw me approach. He screamed, *"NO! Turn the blade flat!"*

Just before I sliced him in two, disgraced by my lack of judgement, I slung the machete into the ground where it came to penetrate upright, and I began squashing and swiping his affliction with my hands. The aborigine came to help. It took the three of us a considerable amount of effort and energy before the pilot was free of them. But the pain inflicted was so severe it lasted throughout that night and part of the next day. It was and is still said these ants are called *"bullet ants"* because their neurotoxic venom produces pain comparable to a gunshot wound…

We did NOT return to the strangler fig. We found several boulders suitable for decent enclosure and decided to spend a few more hours recovering our energy and need for sleep. We took turns napping at brief intervals for several more hours. This time, I did not fail the pilot. I kept my eyes open until it was time for him to keep watch.

Within the approaching twilight, we roused ourselves to continue our trek...

CHAPTER 7

The **WADI**

We eventually reached a ravine through which ran a wadi. Water barely trickled past its stones. Full sunlight had crested behind us and had begun to sweep away shadow from the pinnacle of the mountainous terrain in front of us. The warm hues of late sunrise soon lit the dark jade of the forest toward fulgent malachite. It was then that I noticed how brutal the ant attack had been. The Irishman appeared as a pimpled teenager. Angry red bumps and welts were everywhere…

We'd been soaked by brief tropical storms the past few days every few hours. Although the day had begun with no hint there'd be a storm, it seemed we would not be that lucky.. As we trekked along the crack of the wadi, running a course toward the western horizon, obnubilate darkness crept across the sky. Like the belly of a firefly, the clouds ashen grey would intermittently bloat with demonic orange-grey firelight deep within. Bolts of lightning surged from the clouds. They arborized into tendrils of fire and singed the earth. We knew there would soon be an impenetrable sheet of rain to blanket all beneath it into cryptic opacity.

Arborized tendrils of fire struck all around us. Tornadic winds howled and thrashed the trees. The botanic sea came alive. The water from the cloudburst bled into the ravine of the wadi. A mud avalanche dislodged stones and uprooted trees along the slopes on either side of it.

The wadi filled rapidly. We three and the donkey climbed from the "*pit*" and clung desperately to vines, saplings, roots; anything that'd kept us from being washed back into what no longer was a trickling brook but a raging river. All the while we'd held tight, we'd also protected our friend, the donkey. We'd kept it safely within our grasp.

The storm moved past the ridge of the ravine off into the distant horizon expanding and contracting like the proboscis of a blood sucking mosquito.

The "*river*" that had crept toward our feet quickly ebbed back into a sweltering evaporate as the sun returned. What had been a reasonable path became a mud sump through which we onerously knew we must tread.

It seemed the "*paleolithic*" chief had been correct in his estimate the length of time it'd take to reach the swamp. We would not come to its edge this day...

CHAPTER 8

The DONKEY & the QUAGMIRES

Ironically, despite the benefit, we'd yet to use the donkey! It'd followed behind us. We'd felt too sorrowful toward it. We didn't want to BURDEN the *"beast of burden."* It was too small. We were too big. Its eyes were too pitiful. But our fatigue had become so overwhelming our pace had slowed toward that of a three-legged turtle. So, we implemented the plan we'd yet to use: I'd ride the burro uphill (since I was lighter); the pilot would ride the burro downhill (since he was heavier). Along terrain that was flat neither one of us would ride it so that the beast could *"recover."*

The burro was a woeful ungulate. With stertorous breath it struggled to bear our weight. It'd tug along using the strength of its neck undulations to help propel us forward. Worse, our burden was greater than it ought to have been since the *"equine"* was so short our feet and ankles acted as plows in the mud. Each time I rode it I felt grief for its affliction ~ me!

The trail had become inordinately muddy, and it had been made worse by a cluttering of botanical debris that'd washed onto it from the severity of several recent storms. All this litter made more difficult our need to *"flush out"* any viper hid amongst the tangles. So, more than ever, our eyes kept to the ground beneath our feet and not necessarily directed toward the western horizon. The few times the path had become so indistinct or obstructed we couldn't follow it, our young guide, now with a foot not only bleeding from a gruesome cut but festering purulence from the gash, would bring us back to the proper trail...

In the late afternoon as shadows became less transparent, while it was again my turn to ride the donkey, I suddenly sank into a *"soft spot"* of mud. It came no wider than the trail; only a bit wider than me and the burro. It came with no hint it existed. We were immediately ingurgitated, gulped, sucked into it up to our necks. A membranous pellicle of rotting organic debris, initially spread away by our abrupt entrance, returned to coat our necks as though it were eerily alive.

Immediately I realized we'd been *"imbibed"* by a circumscribed bog...a quagmire. What had engulfed us was no puddle! This *"surprise"* was unlike any I'd ever seen depicted in movies. It wasn't vast. It didn't *"slowly"* consume us. We dropped into it as though it were thin pudding.

I began to fear we'd not reached the quagmire's bottom. We sank a bit further. The mud rose from my neck to my chin. It rose to the donkey's jaw. I slipped off the ungulate I'd been riding to lessen, I hoped, the pressure of our descent.

The pilot and the *"guide"* had walked on not realizing the donkey and I, we, were no longer behind them. The two of them began to disappear as they descended a knoll in the path. And still, they'd remained oblivious to our absence. I thought to yell, but I was so disheartened, depressed, fatigued, sleepy; hungry, I did not. I just watched the Irishman and our guide disappear. I felt sorrow for the donkey. It was wide-eyed and obviously terrified...

Minutes passed...

After a bit, I guess the Irishman realized I and the donkey had disappeared. First, I saw the top of the Irishman's fiery hair as he rose above the knoll heading back along the trail probably hoping to find us but fearing the worst. As he came into full view, I saw he brandished his .44 magnum probably because he'd imagined some animal had attacked us. It wasn't that uncommon for a ravenous beast like a jaguar to rip a person from the trail with such stealth no one realized they were missing.

But then, he saw us, the donkey and I. Slowly, hesitantly, relieved; he sheathed his pistol. He began uproarious laughter, pointed a finger as though he wished he'd had a camera and sauntered blithely toward the quagmire. His demeanor changed as he realized our predicament. With a serious gruffness, he commanded, "*Hand me the reigns of the donkey. Move away from the burro and drag yourself with a slow methodic back paddle to the sumps edge. Heave yourself out from the bog. You and I and the 'native' will then try to drag the donkey out of this pit.*"

Getting the donkey out of the pit was almost impossible despite the three of us giving it great effort. We didn't want the beast to die the way it would have died had we left it there. We did not give up. We kept at it pulling and tugging ~ tugging on the burros' neck; pushing his butt from behind. The beast FINALLY *"bubbled"* and *"sucked"* free from the quagmire.

Although there was no way to interpret the ungulates own emotions during its entrapment, it seemed the donkey had been so traumatized, so terrorized by the event of sinking in mud up to its jaw, it'd gone limp with despair. It didn't lift a *"hoof"* to help us with its escape. But I thought I'd sensed the burro was appreciative our effort to save it (?).

Now, I welcomed the rain. Nothing was then and is now *"ickier"* to me than being coated with drying mud. Fortunately, I didn't have to wait long before the mud was gone, and I was soaked only in fresh water by the event of another powerful storm.

From the quagmire onward, our steps were more measured; more cautious; more wary. But, despite spreading the distance between us and continuously checking to see whether anyone seemed to have *"disappeared"* along the trail, time and again, we'd inadvertently sink into one of those things. The difference was that we had become experienced enough the ordeal of getting out of them had become less burdensome.

We no longer rode the donkey. It had suffered so much terror each time it sank into a quagmire we felt it deserved a break from the additional burden of carrying our weight. But, on occasion, we'd latch onto the donkey's tail to help drag us along the path.

This process continued until dusk was fully upon us. We decided the trail had become too treacherous. There were too many unseen *"quicksand"* sumps. We decided to find shelter. Before the dark of night, we encamped beneath the hollow of a limestone precipice once carved by meteoric water. As before, we took turns sleeping...

CHAPTER 9

HUNGER

My hunger had grown intolerable. Along the trail, I'd begun to chew leaves and twigs. There was no food. The suspected "*anthropophagite*" that guided us had an uncooked corn paddy he knew I'd been staring at from the onset of our trip. While we rested, he noted how pitiful my state. He pulled out his corn paddy, now caked in mud, torn, and with "*growth*" around its edges, and offered it to me. Feeling unworthy of his kindness, I refused it at first. After all, the entire journey the pilot and I had believed he'd eat us if he got the chance. I felt guilt. I felt I didn't deserve his kindness...and...I didn't! But, after several attempts insisting I take it, I shamefully gave in...and...I...ate it...!

At daybreak, a sparkling irradiance could be seen not far from where we'd encamped! Having come down several miles off a gentle slope from the cave, we found ourselves at the edge of a stagnant pool that stretched indistinctly into a haze that concealed its expanse. It was the elusive SWAMP...

As planned, the aborigine who'd managed to guide us to the swamp and NOT eat us, gave a '*'goodbye*'' nod, took the reins of the burro and walked away...

We watched him disappear, then turned toward it, the swamp...

CHAPTER 10

The SWAMP

This morass of particulate opaque water seemed vast. Its furthest edge, if there was one, could not be seen (?). Its depth could not be estimated. What lived within it could only be conjectured from memories of the predatory life I'd read about. The smell of rotting eggs and decaying cabbage permeated its air…

The swamp's water held the flying buttresses of tall, thick tree trunks sporadically scattered ~ some rotting; some with bark torn free by lightning; some not more than burnt stumps. An unctuous pellicle brought by the residual rot of things left unseen and dying coated its surface. Webs weaved by what must have been GIGANTIC SPIDERS lent diaphanous curtains here and there to warn their existence to bat and bird but not to the prey they were meant to ensnare. In all this gloom, a maze of flowering lianas, orchids, colorful bromeliads, and white flowering water lilies brought bright hues to an otherwise dark mist almost impenetrable to sunlight.

Before stepping into this olive morass, I looked down at the edge of its water. I was dismayed to see bubbles rising from its depth. They'd burst at the swamp's edge into ringlets of bilious opacity to briefly disrupt the swamp's rancid cuticle. Within that moment of this "*bubbled clarity,*" mosquito larval hordes could be seen wriggling. Such a sight portended what awaited us when dusk grew near if we were still wading within the waters of the swamp...

I knew our first step into this morass would dilute away the seeping gruel of blood still draining from cuts we'd incurred along the way. I knew that blood would disperse. I knew savage life would awaken and track its source...

Before I took a step into this water, the Irishman grabbed my shoulder and told me to "*pee*" first ~ not in the water but on the embankment. Seeing I was confused by his odd request, he, as was his nature, began a soliloquy:

> *"It is said, within these waters there swims a 'vampiric' fish called the* **Candiru**. *It's a tiny skinny fish that is said to be attracted to urine. As long as you're not submerged in water you're safe. But if you pee in the water, that fish will find you and swim into the canal of your pecker. There it gets stuck and dies. It can only be removed by slicing the 'dick' open. If it is not removed, your pecker eventually will rot and fall off!*
>
> *Of course this is a 'fish tale' of aboriginal legend. It might not be true. But we shouldn't take the chance. Don't pee again,*

if possible, until we reach the end of the swamp...or die from some other beast swimming within these waters...!

Of course, there are things to worry about before we reach solid land~ the snakes, the piranha, the ambush caimans. But those cannot be avoided by simply holding in your pee..."

For a moment, there was silence between us. Before we entered the swamp, before I set a single toe within its predacious water, I emptied my bladder more completely than ever I had before. I prayed we'd reach land before the urge returned.

We'd have preferred to wait until early morning to cross the mire. But we'd arrived near dusk. If we waited until dawn, we'd have lost another day. We believed it was too risky for the Amerindian and Parky to be stuck in the jungle any longer than necessary. We decided to "*take our chances*" by crossing the thing knowing full well, at some point, we'd be in total darkness.

Before our first step, we agreed we'd walk in tandem with me reasonably behind the Irishman. To avoid alerting its predacious water, we'd make as little disturbance as possible and keep our gait as rhythmic as possible. We'd not cough, nor grunt, nor speak, nor "*pee*." All this we'd do until either, one or both of us, had perished or had reached the concealed distant bank. Submerged sometimes only to our knees; at other times, to our necks; caught in the tangle unseen beneath or trapped and sucked into quicksand, we agonizingly inched our way through the swamp...

During the remaining daylight, certain shafts of light penetrating the canopy above allowed us, from time to time, to estimate the sun's arc. We'd hoped to have reached the western edge of the swamp before dusk became night but the vastness before us indicated such hope was a foolish thought. As we traversed this *"wet green incubus,"* our skin began to wrinkle into painful translucent griseous flesh. Our shoes deteriorated. Our socks disintegrated. We began wading barefoot...

Night came. *"Billions"* of *"no see-ums"* began buzzing into our mouth, our nose, our ears. They bit our flesh and brought tinges of pain. Howler monkeys roared contempt above us. The high-pitched sounds of cicadas and locusts became deafening. Bats darted in and out with echolocation *"clicks"* far too near our heads. Giant frogs bellowed a woeful deep baritone chorus. The fumes of the sulfurous water began to singe our nostrils with its nauseous scent and taint bitter our taste buds. Now soaked, coated in olive slime, the night added arctic cold to our torment. I feared my shivering might alert an otherwise dormant beast...

Onward we sloshed our way; we plowed through one hidden entanglement after the other. We sidestepped the vermiculate watery trails heralding the passage of snakes and the eerie splash signaling the nearby presence of caimans. Each submerged bramble that scraped my leg I feared was the first brush of a school of curious piranhas. ALL this, and yet, no harm had come.

There was no chance to nap and no chance to rest. We had to make it to the swamp's western edge or drown...

A hint of dawn finally came and still, we tilled through the muck. Behind us, the aphotic night had lightened into ebullient shades of sunrise bringing the dark of the western horizon toward cerulean blue. Shortly thereafter, full daylight was upon us. It seemed, not far, the sheen of the swamp may have come to an end...

The Irishman suddenly rose out of the water. He stood on solid land! He was TRIUMPHANT with joy ~ but, only for a moment. It seemed he'd plowed through a gigantic spider web! His face held a clinging behemoth black-yellow spider so large even, from a distance, I could see its treacherous fangs elevated toward puncture. He fell into an "*arachnoleptic fit*." At once, his masculine, heroic demeanor was stripped of any noble residue. He danced and flailed all over the place. The scene reminded me the night of the bullet ant attack. Despite near death from fatigue and hunger, I broke into riotous laughter while pointing a finger in his direction. His movement was so tumultuous and erratic, the spider, before it had a chance to inflict a gruesome bite, flipped off into a nearby bush.

I thought to capture this hairy giant spider specimen so spectacular was its appearance, but, I knew I didn't have the energy nor the cunning. I surely would have been pithed myself had I attempted to corner it. And, for all the effort, it was improbable I'd capture it anyway. I lamented its escape as the tarantula's last hairy leg retracted beneath a flurry of forest leaves.

The Irishman seemed not bothered I thought the event funny. He was too tired to emote over it. We now stood at the precipice of our next adventure ~ crossing a field of tall lime- colored grass...

Standing there awhile on dry land at the far western edge of the swamp, now barefoot and sockless (our shoes had been "*worn off*" crossing the swamp), not quite ready to walk on, I began to realize making it through that swamp was as much a "*miracle*" as not having been killed by the plane crash. We hadn't been envenomated by a viper, drowned and "*tenderized*" by a caiman, nor riven to shreds by a ravenous school of savage fish. Our penises had not been parasitized by a candiru ~ our penises were "*safe.*"

Even as I celebrated inwardly our great success at surviving the most treacherous water on earth, I sensed something was missing. I slipped my hand down to my hip. The "*balero,*" now caked in Nicaraguan mud, the toy I'd played with at the Rosita saloon, remained tucked away in my pant pocket. The bottle holding the "*spider-crab*" was still attached by vine to a loop of my jean. But the machete sheath was empty! I'd hoped to keep the machete in memory of our trek (were we to survive). It was then I realized I'd left the machete at the foot of the strangler fig tree. I felt EXTREME disappointment I'd lost a great treasure of tangible memory...

CHAPTER 11

The **DOMINANT** "*Pistolero*"

We now stood past the swamp at the edge of a savannah on a field of tall lime-colored grass. It was a wide canyon nestled between two volcanic slopes. In the far distance, we saw a roughhewn wooden fence, a barn, cows, cuspate horned bulls, and horses. Beyond that, a cabin bearing a smokestack and windows, reflected the light of kerosene lamps and candles. We knew the direction of the "*lodge*" was westerly for the horizon behind us had been brightening toward the pastel blue of daylight and the chatoyant white of the sun.

With bedeviled footsteps, scraping our way through the grass, totally exhausted, we agonizingly headed toward the cabin ignoring the threat of the bulls we passed and whatever may lurk hidden at our feet. By the time we reached the veranda of the cabin, the residual morning mist had totally evaporated, and full daylight had effloresced.

As we stood with blank expressions and lax jaws looking at the cabin's front door, it slowly opened. A man stood in the doorway. He did not speak, but we assumed, by his stature and attitude, he was the owner or foreman of this ranch. He held a shotgun (both barrels loaded), and point it at our bellies...

Before us, a remarkable man stood whose shoulders virtually spread the width of the cabin's door frame. He was tall for a Nicaraguan but still shorter than either of us. He possessed an odd mix of Caucasian features more Spanish than those of true Amerindians. The sun had thickened his skin like that of a pachyderm; his head was chocked full of black hair with occasional strands of grey. There was a scar cut through his right cheek and he bore the curse of once florid acne as testimony to an adolescence long ago forsaken. His eyes were almost black but revealed, by subtilties, an authoritative individual accustomed to being in command. He had grown a thick reddish moustache that wildly poked his upper lip and nose and dangled past his chin to conceal a loose, wrinkled neck. He was muscular, clean, and healthy looking. A *"gaucho"* hat lay at his back held about his neck by its strap. The hat had been bedecked by Macaw feathers and an intricate silver studded ban. A colorful scarf hung around his neck and draped over a loosely buttoned red cotton shirt. A leather belt fitted with silver accents, a silver pistol, and a polished machete hung diagonally from his hip. His pants flared at the thigh and were tucked into calf high leather boots fitted with jingling silver spurs. He seemed an uncompromising, rugged individual; just the kind of guy that could carve a spot out from the jungle and, without much thought, put a bullet in our heads too...!

At first no one spoke. He *"eyed"* us. He seemed skeptical our intent.

Sensing the unease of the situation, the Irishman inarticulately sighed, *"We...crashed..."*

The *"Spaniard's"* demeanor broke from stern confrontation to a huge grin. He lowered the shotgun and set it at the cabin's door frame (but his right hand remained *"rested"* on his holstered pistol). He then laughed and, with an obvious English-Spanish accent, he said, *"Gringos, dos yous knows yous got black tings suckin' yous blood?"*

In concert, we listlessly mumbled, *"No sir, we didn't know we had them things stuck to us..."*

We looked at each other too weary to exhibit emotion. Black slimy looking *"slugs,"* leeches clung all over our skin. Blood dripped from around their *"piercing"* wormy mouths and onto the wooden veranda. We hadn't noticed them; we hadn't felt them.

By this time, we'd become surrounded by several *"ranch hands."* Dressed similar to the *"boss,"* but decked out far less richly, all possessed machetes, pistols, and knives. But instead of shooting us or fatally stabbing us as we first thought they'd do (shooting us would have waisted bullets), the *"boss"* ordered them, instead, to help rid us of the leeches.

We stripped to nakedness. After everyone but us had a good laugh at our pitiful *"gringo"* nudity, the Spaniards became engaged in plucking the sanguine-bloated squishy things from us. In the end, our stark ghostly whiteness, except for the burn of our faces, arms, and legs, contrasted sharply with the black and bloody pile of wormy beasts wriggling at our feet. In that the "*worms*" possessed an anticoagulant in their spit (hirudin), though they had been ripped from our flesh and we should have clotted shortly thereafter, we continued to trickle blood for several hours.

The foreman could see the two of us had no humanity left. We were shoeless, soaked in swamp sweat, caked in mud, and stood gaunt with expressionless, dull-eyed, gapping, crack-lipped faces. We were unshaven and smelled feculent with a touch of rotten egg. Our hair clung to our skulls in tangled rivulets and crawled with tiny flea-like bugs. Bruises, cuts; scrapes knit through our skin. And, of course, we dripped with blood both curdled and trickling.

As though perplexed with profound indecision about what next to do with the two of us, hemming and hawing, he finally, resolutely, demanded we wash ourselves in his horse trough. This we did but without soap. We also soaked and wrung out our tattered clothes. Since we were beyond worrying about being killed in our sleep we each took a brief nap. Oddly, it did not occur to us to ask for food… and none was given.

The morning had dragged toward noon before we had a chance to thank the foreman for his generosity (He hadn't stabbed nor shot us.). The Irishman then bartered another deal.

For a substantial price (the entire money roll left in the Irishman's pocket), the foreman would let us "*borrow*" two reigned but unsaddled horses. Two of his ranch hands would lead us to a town called Matagalpa where there should be a telegraph we could use to contact Managuan authorities to provide rescue. According to the *"boss,"* this leg of our harsh journey, if by horse, should not take more than one or two more days…

CHAPTER 12

The "Death Knell" By **HORSEBACK**

The foreman was as covetous of his horses and tack as was the jungle covetous of its food. He provided us only with reins. We rode bareback. The Irishman and I trotted off from the ranch with two of his *"saddled cowboys"* maintaining a westerly direction over well-worn narrow paths through the grass and the jungle.

The path, for the most part, was easy compared to what we'd experienced the past few days. In fact, the rhythmic clopping of the horse hooves sent us off into sleep throughout the course of the day. We'd suddenly awake with a startled jerk whenever our sleep so deepened we began to slip off the beasts. At least the steed's height did not force us to drag our feet along the path and, at least, they were big enough (about seventeen hands high) we didn't feel too heavy a burden on their backs.

The topography undulated between hills and valleys; some very steep; some shallow. There were occasions when the jungle encroachment was so great we'd have to walk leading our horses grueling distances before the trail once again became rideable. Occasionally, especially when we lulled off to sleep, we'd get slugged by a tree branch or scraped by an intruding giant boulder. But we encountered no more quagmires and throughout the entire day no rain fell. We were certain, with the improved speed of travel on horseback, the last leg of our journey would take only one day instead of two...

We had been ascending a gradual slope almost the entire day. I judged, by the sun's position, it must have been nearing three o'clock in the evening before we'd reached its summit. Our horses broke through a narrow slit between two towering, jagged granite monoliths bedecked by a cluster of white boulders, a couple of straggly trees and a patch of sickly grass. And then, the trail vanished. We'd reached an edge with an upward slant beyond which nothing could be seen save a cloudless pale blue sky...?

The horse's seemed frightened. They became wide-eyed and began to stressfully whinny and leap about uncontrollably. I thought there must be a snake at their hoofs, but instead, it was because we'd reached the precipice of a cliff! We'd traveled the entire day upward only to meet a cliff! I was extremely aggravated. I, at first, thought this meant we'd have to retrace our trail. Were we forced to do that; our entire day would have been waisted! The pilot and I turned toward the gauchos furious they'd not known about this impasse...

The cowboys seemed unaffected by our demeanor. Seeing our irritation, the two of them were grinning with faces unshaven and tanned to near blackness. Their gold teeth sparkled with delight. While nonchalantly leaning forward on the pommels of their saddles, they seemed well pleased with themselves.

The lead *"cowboy"* then spoke, *"Yous boys fraid somthin'?"* He spurred his horse and motioned we follow him to the edge of what we'd thought a vertical precipice. He then roguishly commanded, *"We go down...follow..."* I was confused. Did he really mean we were to drop past this ledge? The thought of it petrified me...

CHAPTER 13

The RAVINE

While we cowardly pondered what fate might bedevil us if we were to drop past what seemed oblivion, the *"gauchos"* themselves were undaunted. They spurred their horse's flanks and shot over the ledge and precipitously out of sight! Immediately, we dismounted our horses and warily, but rapidly, walked to the cliff 's precipice…

We found ourselves starring at the brink of a perilous drop. At least it wasn't vertical. It presented as a slant of about seventy degrees that stretched the length of two football fields. It seemed the *"gauchos"* were sliding down an avalanche chute of loamy dirt pouring from the cliff 's apogee toward a raging *"white water"* river cascade at the end of the descent. Seeing this, we simultaneously whispered, *"You've got to be kidding…?"*

We weren't exactly skilled horsemen and our horses had already demonstrated their fear. But we knew we were to follow these two guys if there was any chance we'd survive. Fortunately; mimicry is a characteristic inherent in primates. Before doing something stupid, we first observed the *"cowboys"* method of descent:

The two *"gauchos"* immediately leaned back toward the rump of their horses and had then let the ungulates take command. The horses maintained a sliding descent with their rumps plowed into the scree and their hooves and fetlocks stretched straight forward to counterbalance their descent. While holding a double hand grip on the saddle's pommel, the gauchos had leaned back against the *"cantle"* of their saddle almost horizontal to the slant of the *"cliff"* and they'd brought their feet out of the stirrups straight toward the mandible of the horse. The gaucho's descent had been straight as an arrow. When they'd dropped into the river below, they dismounted their horses and grabbed their steed's manes. The ungulates then navigated the raging river diagonally crossing it without difficulty. Although the two men were pulled by the current until rounding a bend beyond our sight, it seemed reasonable to assume they'd made it to the other side of the river.

Seeing this, we didn't immediately copy it. Instead, we waited to see whether the cowboys and their horses reappeared. If there was no evidence they'd *"made it,"* we determined we'd find another way.

Within a matter of several apprehensive minutes, the *"cowboys,"* now not more than two dots at the river's furthest edge, soaked but unscathed, reappeared. They waved us onward...

At eighteen, I was more foolish than brave. I volunteered to go first but the Irishman felt I should wait to see how it went with him. After all, although the cowboys had *"made it,"* they had saddles ~ we were bareback. It didn't take much for him to convince me this was the best plan. He hopped on his unsaddled horse and shot over the precipice. At first it seemed his path down the chute would be no different than the *"cowboys,"* but halfway he fell off his horse. The horse continued onward, hit the river, and as had the other horses, seemed to navigate the river without difficulty.

The Irishman, now dethroned, rode the rest of the landslide on his butt, struck the river, navigated downstream with his feet directed downstream, and seemed to take the currents at a diagonal. But he too soon disappeared behind a bend as had everyone else. I made no movement. I waited to see whether the fighter pilot had made it…

Not long thereafter, the Irishman rejoined the two *"gauchos."* Now, the three of them looked up to see my tiny, distant image. *"COME ON!,"* the pilot seemed to entice though I couldn't hear him.

I do have a fear of heights. And this avalanche of scree was so steep it seemed a vertical precipice to me. I was terrified. But everyone else had survived and my eighteen-year-old priapic pride could not let itself be gutless. So, scared beyond belief, I hopped on my horse, gave it a kick in its flank and over we went. I imitated all that I'd observed regarding riding this chute, but the horse struck a root shortly after the beast and I had dropped from the precipice. Headfirst we went into a somersaulting tumble. I grabbed its mane with both hands and let loose the reigns to avoid tugging on the horse's neck in an untoward fashion.

I squeezed its flanks as tight as my thighs would allow. The two of us, the horse and I, continued down the dirt slide tumbling head over heels again and again. I'd get buried beneath the dirt the second the beast's back crushed into the earth. I'd hold my breath. When the horse again came upright, I gasp for another breath ~ and so on…over and over…

It was probably VERY stupid not to have dismounted at the top of the cliff when the horse first tripped, but I didn't. We, the horse, and I, "*cartwheeled*" all the way into the river.

When I hit the river, I was dislodged. The horse swam on. Before I could right myself, I struck a fallen tree and became momentarily compressed against its tangle of branches. Looking across the river I could see the cowboys and the Irishman yelling, gesturing, but I could not hear what they were saying or what their gestures meant. Having watched the Irishman drift down river, I knew it must be wise to travel the white water feet first to protect my head and I reasoned he must have crossed the river on a slant to navigate the currents to reach the opposite bank. Knowing this, of course, did me no good. I was trapped within a flurry of branches, its eddy, and simultaneously compressed toward asphyxiation. The current eddy kept dragging me again and again beneath its water. I was drowning…

Desperate, I knew I couldn't keep getting dragged beneath the water much longer. It occurred to me to take a chance and let myself drop under all this turbulence hoping I might be lucky and discover an alternative escape from my mortal predicament. I reasoned the swirl of an eddy is similar to a toilet flush. I reasoned the bottom of a "*toilet flush swirl*" seemed to "*spit out*" what had been contained within it. I also knew, if I allowed myself to drop beneath the eddy, it might be the last breath I'd take. But, the way it was going, I thought I would soon drown anyway...

I released my grasp on the branches and sank into the whirlpool. I began spinning downward like a corkscrew. But I kept my eyes open. Looking into the roiling bluish-white water with each pass that would direct me downstream, I spotted an irregular gap amongst the arborizing limbs of the fallen tree as I simultaneously struck the bedrock of the river. From this, I pushed off into the downstream direction of this infundibular pipe.

By pure chance, the current shot me through a gap of entanglement as though I were a torpedo. I resurfaced free from my nemesis, directed my feet downstream and paddled diagonally across the raging river cascades until I came to the shallows of the opposite bank about a half mile downstream.

Bruised and bleeding, I immediately notice the two *"gauchos"* were saddled waiting for me while the Irishman trotted to where I stood, leapt from his horse, and helped drag me off the muddy embankment.

The two *"cowboys"* appeared incredibly angry...?

Although I didn't speak Spanish, the Irishman interpreted what they were blustering. It seemed, when they retrieved my riderless horse, they discovered I'd torn loose one of its rains during my attempt to survive. I'd ruined their bosses' bridle. They'd become *"spittin' mad,"* red faced mad, red- eyed mad, and inconsolably mad! I thought they were going to shoot me! Had it not been for the Irishman's presence, his hand prepared to pull his .44 magnum, and his demeanor prepared to blow them off their saddles, maybe, they would have shot me…? Instead, they grabbed our two horses and rode off leaving us stranded at the bank of the river…

CHAPTER 14

ABANDONED!

As the two *"gauchos"* strode away and left us abandoned, one muttered through clenched teeth, *"The outpost, Matagalpa, is just over the next escarpment…"*

Still drenched from my ordeal and the excitement from the threat of getting a bullet hole driven into my encrusted, barnacled, lethargic brain, I paused to note the significance of the last hour of our misadventure. I marveled the improbability either the Irishman or me were still alive. Root loops of the scree could have torn free our ligaments; outcrops of stone along the descent could have cracked our skulls; the tumbling horse could have burst our ribs and punctured our lungs; the river could have drowned us! But none of this happened! As before, all these dire *"should haves"* kept me believing, as improbable as it then seemed, the reason I'd kept surviving these deadly events was that *"God"* had spared my life so that, someday, I'd achieve my ultimate destiny: To become a surgeon...

Barefoot, washed clean by the river; draped in tattered wet clothes, wounds finally coagulated, we set about heading west toward our *"Oz,"* the *"outpost"* ~ Matagalpa…

Now afoot, we headed west toward the *"next escarpment."* Rising above the riverbank, we were met by a flat field of barren, dwarfed, twisted, grey-white trees. They grew within white quartz sand that sparkled like a sea of diamonds. The field stretched to the base of a vertical limestone escarpment. At the summit of this bluff stood an isolated gnarly tree backlit by the sun. If we could successfully scale the precipice, we decided this tree would be our marker to continue west…

By nightfall we'd reached the base of the crag. By then we'd become severely dehydrated. Within a narrow fissure there trickled water. We drank..

Bedraggled, hungry, weak, gaunt, somnolent, blistered, baked, scabbed, and trickling blood afresh, looking up, the escarpment we faced seemed to have no end. We considered *"giving up."*

But we knew not finding rescue meant killing Parky and the *"Mayan."* In desperation, not certain whether we could endure the climb, we began our ascent…_

Snaking our way past one impasse after another, slipping, loosing grip, collapsing onto one crevice to the next, getting cut and bruised, loosing breath, and having to pause, we ever so gradually continued upward. Well into the night, we climbed…

As the climb took its toll on our strength, as the hours came and went; as we ascended higher, the need to sleep became overwhelming! But we **COULD NOT SLEEP**! ~ if sleep came, we'd be dispatched from the cliff! Ironically, knowing this, in a way, gave us added resolve to keep going...

As daybreak seemed eminent, we finally came to the peak of the escarpment. We spotted our *"compass"* tree and began our journey once again heading west. We'd hoped the village of Matagalpa would be encountered just beyond the cliff ~ it was not. At first there didn't seem to be a path that a least indicated it might lead to Matagalpa. But, as we approached the rise of the jungle beyond the cliff, a clear- cut path was revealed. We reasoned such a well-worn path would not have been found unless it had been made by the people of Matagalpa. We followed it. Evening came. Night came. Still the path continued on with no hint the village was near...

There came a very faint, far off light. It flickered as though lit by electricity. It appeared to the left of the trail. We assumed it must come from the village of Matagalpa. We diverged from the path and headed toward the light.

The terrain from the path was precarious. It was full of pits, quagmires, hillocks, shallow ravines, sump holes, rivulets, and entanglements of vine and bush all uncut and untamed by human presence.

Realizing the light was bound to vanish then reappear as we crossed the mutability of this landscape, we created a novel method of advancing toward it. We decided to *"leapfrog"* our advance. I'd stand at the rise of one hill sighting the light while the Irishman climbed to the next; then, he'd sight the light while I advanced forward to where he stood...and...so on...

As we came nearer, more lights were seen ~ two, three; four…

Then the lights went out! (In the jungle there is a paucity of electricity. This issue is resolved by shutting off the power well before the next dawn.)

We now stood paralyzed by the abyssal dark. Our brains, beset by starvation and somnolence, began to fear the *"imps of hallucination"* might have tricked us ~ perhaps there had never been any light...?

But, light or no light, it made no difference. If that light had not been our guide, if Matagalpa wasn't near, we were *"finished"* anyway...

So, we continued to move forward...

CHAPTER 15

MATAGALPA

Dawn began to cast away the darkness; to brighten the jungle. We began hearing the snort of a horse, the bellow of a cow; a rooster's morning crow. We passed broken artifacts of tools dispersed from chronic wear and tear. And, at the top of a hill, there appeared a grassless muddy clearing staid from the dense jungle like the scalp of a tonsured monk! It held a few depauperate eighteenth century *"Churrigueresque"* stucco buildings separated by a wide, guttered street of muddy puddles. A few native thatched huts rimmed the main buildings. There were hitching posts. Electric wires were strung atop stone-cut wood poles. And there were several streetlamps!

We'd arrived at Matagalpa!

The Irishman suggested I rest near one of the *"hitching posts"* while he searched the town for its *"fabled"* telegraph.

My eyes were burning with intolerable pain. Blinking made it worse. My eyelids might as well have been stung by a wasp! I was as near complete exhaustion as I'd believed possible without dying. And now, now that it seemed rescue was certain, my brain completely shut down. I collapsed into a puddle onto my extended right arm and SLEPT!

I don't know how long my sleep lasted but the Irishman said, when he returned from his hunt for a telegraph, he feared, as he came upon me lying in the street more an immobile heap of *"garbage"* than a thing human, I'd died! It was only when I took a sonorous breath he realized I lived. He tried to wake me.

I recall feeling my body shaken by a massive hand tugging on my shoulder. I heard shouting, cajoling, begging. A masculine voice said, *"get up."* I wanted to respond, but I didn't; I couldn't. It seemed all this aggravating nuisance was coming from a dream ~ NOT reality. The voice seemed far off, distant, a muted echo within a tunnel. It seemed a voice conflated within the nightmares I was experiencing arisen from the depravity of my sleep; the insanity of my starvation! But, as the annoying voice continued to resonate in my ears and the jiggling of my shoulder became more aggressive, a degree of wakefulness began to intrude on the content of my bizarre dreams ~ I began to return to the real world. Yet, still, I seemed paralyzed. My lips didn't move despite my effort to respond to the voice that intruded. I faded in and out of consciousness...

I slipped back to sleep and with that, a bizarre dream emerged:

> I dreamt I sat in the chair of my white-haired, wrinkled, bent, bespeckled dentist's office ~ the arcane office

with the "*sewing machine*" drill whose peddle the dentist had to "*pump*" with his foot to get it to "*drill*"; the kind where pain was excruciating; the kind often built over the top of apothecaries of the 1950's with lighting that of gloom; the kind with windows open and NO air conditioning; the kind invaded by flies during the summer.

I saw myself as I was when I was eight. I dreamt the dentist had bent over me holding a cloth to my face. He was anesthetizing me with chloroform gas (The same gas I used for bugs!). Unfortunately, for me, my childhood teeth were so "*rotten*," I dreamt I'd experienced this "*treatment*" MANY times!

The gas always induced a peculiar distortion of my reality. Each time the dentist inflicted me with chloroform gas, as I went "*under*," a strange idiosyncratic optic illusion surfaced. I began to see a white "*optic spiral*" emerge within the dark of my brain. It was the kind used by hypnotists. It first arose as a translucent "*black and white disk*" gradually spiraling with greater intensity as it became more opaque. As the gas separated my brain from reality, I felt my senses diminish asymptotically toward oblivion.. Then time ceased...

My "*dentist*" dream did not end there:

I dreamt, as I awoke from my "*chloroform*" anesthesia I was stricken by extreme nausea. I dreamt my teeth had been *"cured"* but I was permanently *"toothless."* Still, trapped within this illusion, I began to wonder why the dentist looked exactly like... the Irishman (?).

The transmutation of the old bent dentist into that of the tall brute of an Irishman startled me. It brought me FULLY awake!

I wasn't in the dentist's office at all. I was a *"maladroit"* lying in a rancid, feculent, muddy puddle filled with whirligigs, water boatmen, and wiggly mosquito larvae. As the restraints of my *"dream state"* shed toward greater clarity, my senses returned. Of these, the most intense was **PAIN**!

Every one of my bones had contracted into an arthritic posture; every joint felt aflame with unbearable pain. Now more awake, I realized my right arm, the one I'd laid against, was STILL immobile. It was totally numb. My arm seemed not a part of me; it did not seem attached.

I became recklessly irrational. Hysterically, I rose from the mud puddle and ran throughout the streets of Matagalpa pitifully lifting my limp right arm scowling, *"My arm is dead! My arm is dead! I'm rotting!"*

Looking back over my shoulder, as the Irishman diminished in perspective as I ran with no end point considered, I could see he was uproariously laughing with an expression of incredulity. He wasn't concerned in the least I was about to die. So, I stopped running. Gasping for air, I walked back to where I'd left him. My expression was one of betrayal. I didn't understand how he could be so composed. Couldn't he see I was in trouble?

The World War II fighter pilot continued NOT to be concerned (?). He was a rugged, romantic, adventurer but NOT a doctor. However, he'd encountered such ailments before and, still unbeknown to me, he knew I'd soon discover my *"ailment."* He knew it was only temporary. He knew, once I realized that, I'd probably be consumed with great embarrassment.

Looking down at me as though he was my true father, he soothed my apprehension. He said, *"You're not going to rot! Your arm fell asleep by laying on it. It'll come around. It's not dead! Give it a few more minutes."*

As we stood in silence for a bit, he broke the mood by informing me he'd found a telegraph. In a professorially *"matter-of-fact"* tone, he said, *"I've contacted the Managua military. They'll be here soon. They're coming to rescue us. Some of them will head into the jungle to retrieve Parky and the 'Mayan.'"*

As he spoke, my arm began to awaken. Even though *"pins and needles"* shot down the limb with electric sensitivity, I was immensely relieved. So intense was the shock produced by the slightest pressure, it took over an hour before the paresthesia subsided enough I could touch or lift anything without going into a dramatic *"theatrical spastic jig."*

I noticed the Irishman, when he'd returned to retrieve me, had held a yellow hibiscus flower in his hand the entire time we'd been together in Matagalpa. When my head finally cleared its *"cobwebs,"* I asked him why? In a deep, soft, masculine voice, he said:

"When I saw this flower, its wanton blonde beauty reminded me of your mother. She's on her way with the troops coming to rescue

us. It seems she'd been made aware our plane crash; our disappear-
ance. She flew down to find us. When the authorities were notified
our presence in Matagalpa, she was invited to come with them.
This flower is my gift to her ~ to let her know, even during our
deadly ordeal, I had but one thought: to survive so that I could
see her one more time..."

On mother's arrival, the World War II fiery-haired, ragged, dirtied, barefooted fighter pilot genuflected as any knight at the table of King Author. Lowering his head, he raised the arm carrying *"her"* flower, and asked, *"Will you consecrate this flower?"*

Mother nearly fainted from the romance of his gesture. Trembling, she pressed the flower to her heart...

"**TARZAN**" *& the "PILOT."* **Out from the JUNGLE ~ 1966**

Part VI

The **Return** *to* **AMERICA**

Out *of the* JUNGLE

I returned to Kansas City and continued to cohabitate with the Irishman's daughter ~ the one I'd fought so hard to win...

The Rescue of **PARKY** *& the* **"*MAYAN* "**

Within a few days, we were informed Parky, and the "*Mayan*" had been rescued alive and unharmed. But the plane had been hopelessly mired and doomed to rust into antiquity at the edge of the jungle cornfield.

The **VIRTUAL RETURN** *to the* **CRASH SITE**

Fifty years later, I was working as a surgeon. I became aware another surgeon worked at the same hospital I attended. He was from Nicaragua!

I found him and briefly related my adventure. I told him I'd always wanted to return to the site of the plane crash, but such a thing would have caused a tremendous burden. The Nicaraguan surgeon was familiar with everything I described: The cities; the topography.

I was not familiar with the ability to connect to a *"Geographic Information Satellite."* He *"clicked"* onto a *"live overview"* of Nicaragua. We *"scanned"* and *"zoomed in"* on the land between Porte Cabezas and Matagalpa. No hint of the plane or the cornfield could be seen.

More astonishing, the land between those two cities as well as Managua, revealed no *"metastasis"* of civilization; no conurbation despite 50 years had passed since the crash. The cities had remained discretely tucked into the same *"tonsured"* areas as I'd remembered them.

The **DESECRATION** *of an* Entomologist's **DREAM**

I'd lost ALL the insects I'd captured in the jungle except for the arachnid I'd stored in the *"killing jar"* strapped to my hip with a vine. That jar I'd managed, miraculously, to protect. It'd held what I once thought was an undiscovered bug, the bug I'd called a *"spider-crab"*; the bug I was going to name *"Arachnotarzanis tarzanii."* Of course, I eventually discovered the *"arachnid"* was a known arthropod from the order Amblypygi, an order well established that includes 17 genera and 155 species fondly referred to by entomologists as *"whip spiders"* or *"tailless whip scorpions."*

To a novice, as surely I was when I encountered it, this **GIANT** *"bug"* appeared to be a dangerously foul vinegar smelling creature capable of inflicting painful venomous wounds like its spider relatives. But I later discovered it had no venom and it was essentially harmless. Even though I'd learned the "*spiderish -crabish*" bug was not "*toxic*" I still couldn't bring myself to pick it up with my hand. The thing was too ugly and too scary!

When I arrived home, I immediately unpacked the "*killing jar*" holding captive the "*spider-crab.*" I'd left the jar "*airtight*" the entire time after we'd crashed. With anxious anticipation, I unscrewed the lid. "*Death scent*" vapors gasped explosively from the bottle worse than that of foul breath. I was immediately repulsed. I gagged and dashed the jar out from the room into the open air. I let its content evaporate to dryness before again approaching the jar. Although the odor persisted, it was no longer pervasive. Having dried within its own bodily exudates, it'd become "*glued*" to the bottle. I used a blunt spoon to release it. I carefully "*poured*" it from the jar onto a sheet of paper expecting it to remain intact, but it broke into a "*zillion*" pieces except for its eyes. Its eight expressionless piceous eyes starred back…

At that time I was still an amateur "*entomologist*" too limited in knowledge regarding arthropod preservation. After grieving the loss of this bug's integrity, I couldn't think of a way to salvage it. In the days that passed, the bug sat collecting dust in a heap unbecoming. Disheartened, I finally made a "*funeral pyre*" and wrapped the bug in reverent "*mortcloth.*" With a "*sanctified*" wooden match I immolated it to amorphous ash and vapor. Whatever soul persisted within it soon dispersed into the air…

For years I regretted not keeping the spider's body parts, if for no other reason, it represented one of the most adventurous moments of my life. As I became more knowledgeable regarding insect preparation, I eventually learned how to *"repair"* broken bugs and *"reanimate"* them effectively. After acquiring that knowledge, each time I prepared or repaired an insect, the *"scab"* of that *"spider-crab"* experience resurfaced into melancholic memory.

An Ecuadorian Theatre in QUITO

I'm embarrassed to admit that I'd ruminated about the loss of that *"whip spider"* for years. I'd dreamt I'd return to the jungle one day and capture another one...

The first opportunity to return to a *"real"* jungle came again in the mid- 1980's. We, my wife, and I, were to head into Quito, Ecuador, spend a night, then traipse down the slopes of the Andes Mountains, *"catch"* a thirty foot dugout canoe at Lago Agrio, and then head east along the headwaters of the Amazon River until we crossed the border into the Brazilian Amazon Basin. We'd spend the month. We'd collect insects. I hoped to find a *"whip spider"* greater than any I'd ever seen!

While in Quito my wife and I had become bored. We'd decided to saunter lazily along the uneven *"mountainous"* topography of the city. We were in the old part; the part where cobbled streets abound, and buildings reflect romantic antiquities of an era long past. Gas streetlamps brought halos of mystical light and made crystalline the wetness brought by the dew fallen upon the stones of the capricious streets. At that hour of our walk, there was a thin purplish haze that'd layered not only over the city but extended along the base of the Andes distant from the city. Within the horizon to the southwest, as evening headed toward dusk, the mountain's white capped peaks could be seen caught bright by the last embers of the sun but cast in pale violet shadow along their lower slopes.

We came upon a massive "*cathedralesque*" theatre. Its entrance was secured by giant double doors made of well-worn wood bedecked by worrisome splinters. A small window had to be knocked upon before entry. Here, when the proprietor opened the window, for a small fee we could enter. We came into an "*acre*" enclosure covered by a dusty dirt floor upon which dry rot benches festooned with moss had been placed. A screen as large as those seen at drive-in theatres had just begun to show a "*jungle*" movie. Despite knowing we were about to witness a "*VERY LOW budget*" movie...we stayed. The enclosure was echoic. The acoustics were terrible. Even though the script was in "*dubbed*" English, we could not understand what was being said.

When we arrived, the opening credits for the movie had already been shown as well as its title. But, since we were headed into a jungle shortly thereafter, we thought it'd be great fun to watch it...

Rape, cannibalism, mutilation, and torture by a tribe of natives unknown to civilization had been scripted to "*inspire*" the minds of jungle enthusiasts. Having had enough of this movie, we rose to leave. Just then, there appeared a HUGE "*whip-spider*" on the screen of the movie, crawling over a thicket of mud and grass! I hadn't seen that creature since I'd escaped the jungle of Nicaragua. That scene alone made the movie worthwhile!

What are the odds?

The night before we began our journey into the jungle hoping to find another giant whip spider, we'd inadvertently happened upon a theatre showing a movie that had a scene of the VERY BUG WE SOUGHT ~ a **GIANT WHIP SPIDER**!

Amazingly, even the Amblypygid of theatrical production had not been as large as the one I'd captured beneath the burned bark of a Kapok tree! But, the movie gave me hope, somewhere along the banks of the Amazon; perhaps within a limestone cave, or the hollow of a fallen tree trunk, or beneath a stone, I'd find the replacement for the *"infamous"* arthropod of my lament. It didn't happen...

When we returned to the states, I tried to find the movie we'd seen in Quito. But I didn't know its title nor who directed it. So, I bought about ten ridiculously lousy *"D"* grade jungle movies. I suffered through their entirety hoping to see the scene with the *"tailless whip spider."* After ridiculous hours of watching movies that should never have been made I came upon the one I sought. The movie we'd watched in Quito was Umberto Lenzi's HORROR CLASSIC, banned in 31 countries, called, *"Cannibal Ferox."* For its time, it truly was a gruesome movie. But, compared to movies made today, the severity of its *"horror"* and *"sexuality"* would probably get a *"G"* rating!

JUNGLE ROT

One month after the Nicaraguan Adventure, I'd entered college hoping to do well enough some medical school might accept me. Toward that end, my major was biology and chemistry. I was amid taking a *"lab practical"* identifying zoological specimens. We were to walk a circular display of *"critters"* and identify them. Half through this exam, I suddenly sensed a disease prodrome. Things weren't right with my body. A chill began to consume me. I felt I was *"burning up."* A florid sweat soaked my clothes. I began to swoon.

All at once I felt the need to simultaneously defecate and vomit. Without explanation to the professor, I barely completed the exam before rushing from the lab to a nearby bathroom. Simultaneously I vomited and released hemorrhagic diarrhea. Shortly thereafter, my mouth became inflamed, my teeth began to ache, and my throat became lumpy with painful lymph nodes...

I couldn't eat. I continued to periodically vomit and release bloody diarrhea. My conditioned rapidly worsened...

Medical diagnostic tests confirmed I'd been parasitized by Giardia lamblia. It can cause severe *"giardiasis"* diarrhea. In addition to Giardia, I'd also acquired parasitation by Entamoeba histolytica . This is a microscopic anaerobic (does not need oxygen to survive) parasite that causes a bloody form of diarrhea called *"amoebic dysentery."* It is more dangerous than Giardia in that it can enter the blood stream and affect other organs ~ especially, the liver.

A week after the initial symptoms, I'd begun to hemorrhage from my gums. In addition, my tongue and the inner lining of my cheeks began to ulcerate. This condition was called *"Acute Necrotizing Ulcerative Gingivitis"* or *"Trench Mouth"* ~ an infection that occurs generally by an overgrowth of several "*normal*" mouth bacteria (primarily anaerobic and spirochete types) allowed to proliferate during physical stress, starvation, malnutrition, and immune suppression.

It took well over a month of medication before I recovered completely from the sequelae of having not quite escaped the jungle's curse....

Since that "*adventure*," my wife and I have been to numerous jungles. Never again were our bodies invaded by these deadly "*marauders*." Not only did we protect ourselves with appropriate vaccinations, but we also didn't drink "*dangerous*" water, we didn't eat fruits or vegetables soaked in water from the tap, we didn't brush our teeth with water from the tap, and we didn't eat meat not cooked to "*charcoal*."

POSTSCRIPT

SUICIDE

Some may wonder why a child of six would so idealize the story of *"Tarzan and His Mate"*; why that same child would then search for his idealized *"Jane."* Well, like most childhood things, it all began with Mother…

This *"necklace"* of connected destinies or concatenations NEVER would have occurred had I not been aware mother's lifelong despair ~ her need to find *"true love,"* that is, as she defined it, *"an everlasting, incontrovertible, all-consuming perfect blending of the souls."*

As I grew toward manhood it never escaped me mother had never found a man to share her life as she'd dreamt it ought to be. She'd spent her life pining for such a man. It is the probable reason I had many fathers. It is the reason she seemed never to find enduring purpose.

I felt constant sorrow for her. I tried to lift her unhappiness by being the best I could be. But there was no achievement by me, no matter how spectacular, that could elevate her burden. She suffered an inexorable undercurrent; a leitmotif of loneliness never fulfilled. She searched for "*true love.*" Without it she remained a lost soul…

Ultimately, by middle age, despite Mother's own unique attractiveness and innate intelligence, she had given into the despair she felt, the loneliness suffered by never having yet found what she desperately sought ~ a "*soulmate.*"

By my seventeenth year, almost two years before my "*Jane*" escaped her treacherous Stepfather and I met the Irish World War II fighter pilot, the man that ultimately came to fulfill Mother's dream of finding a soulmate, she attempted suicide:

On a day set within the arctic chill of November, I sat in a high school class. I was seventeen. The principal had announced a terrific snowstorm approached the city. He felt it was dangerous enough that, within a few more hours, the roads would be impassable. He announced we were to be released from our classes to return home. This meant I'd be home several hours before Mother expected to see me.

As I approached our meager home, I felt an intense aura portending tragedy. Entering the house, though it should have been bright during the afternoon of the day, I found it had been severely beclouded into darkness by the storm and the fact no light was lit. This brought my heart to pounding with fear something was eerily wrong. A headache, more severe than ever I'd yet experienced, began to bring my head into insufferable pain so severe my vision blurred. There was an intense greasy, nauseous, morbid smell. It seemed it emanated from a low-lying mist that permeated the room where I stood. I heard a *"rumbling"* beneath my feet ~ in the garage below.

No longer capable of standing at the front room entrance, I dispatched myself back into the snow-covered grass; back into the cold; back into a white blizzard now howling its torment.

My headache, after a few intense breaths, evaporated.

Pulled by an innate sense of *"knowing without knowing,"* an ability evolved from the confluence of our senses toward survival, I was compelled to investigate the *"rumbling"* I'd heard from beneath the floor of the living room. Robotically, dazed by mystery, I walked from the yard onto the driveway and slid down its icy slope to the back of the house where the garage had been built; from where the *"rumbling"* came. I hesitantly walked to the garage door...

The garage door had three rectangular windows. All three had been coated with a thin layer of ice framed by accumulated snow. Brushing the snow away,

I peered into the garage. The room was filled with a thick cinereous haze. All was grey except a red hose emerging from our car's exhaust pipe to a narrowly opened driver's seat window. And, in the front seat, was a shock of yellow hair (?).

Again, "*knowing without knowing*," I sensed it was Mother. I lifted the garage door and walked to the driver's seat of the car. The torment of my headache resumed. There, in the car, slumped Mother. Drool from her mouth. No breath in her lungs. I had no idea the "*silent death*" of "*gas fumes*." I did not know about carbon monoxide poisoning. I'd never heard of suicide by this method nor how to accomplish such a thing. But, I knew, if it caused me such pain simply by breathing it for a few seconds, it must have been lethal for Mother.

I pulled her limp, breathless body from its intended tomb, the car, and I dragged it face up onto the snowy grass of the yard. Standing over her body, I thought she was dead.

As I stared at her, it began to dawn on me I was looking at suicide. Worse, I began to realize she'd planed this "*suicide*" so that I'd find her after death had taken its toll. Purely by chance, the school had let out early.

The implications of this event registered slowly. I became NOT sad, but ANGRY. It was dishearteningly clear to me she was so enthralled with her self-imposed, neurotic misery derived from not finding her "*soulmate*," she'd decided life was not worth living. I realized a thing I had not been aware until that moment: she cared for only herself. As I stood decidedly afflicted with this depressing realization, she gasped a breath. After turning to vomit clear gastric fluid; after several paroxysmal fits of coughing, she reached a hand for me to help her rise to her feet. As I took her hand and looked into her weeping, bloodshot eyes, I felt abandoned. I felt orphaned. I felt alone.

My sailor-pharmacist "*Dad*" had already "*orphaned*" me in the sense he'd shown me no interest once he realized Mother no longer showed him interest. I'd long ago realized, since I wasn't really his "*son*" and his relationship with my mother had deteriorated, he'd begun to resent me rather than be proud of me.

The day of her attempted suicide, I knew whatever destiny awaited my future would be welded only by me. I decided I would continue the charade of a dedicated son to his mother and my Stepfather...for her sake. I decided not to let her know I knew the true meaning of this event. I did not reveal my anger, my resentment, or my lack of pity for her suicide attempt. I feigned what was socially acceptable.

Although, at seventeen, I was unaware the psychiatrist Jung had theorized the phenomenon of synchronicity, I did sense the improbability of finding Mother before death was a "*miracle*" ~ an indication of God; a hint there existed a universe sentient and omniscient.

Had Mother not had this flaw, that is, an inability to recognize men for whom she could live *"happily ever after,"* had I not been capable of recognizing, even at six years old, this flaw as the source of her unhappiness and misery, the movie, *"Tarzan & His Mate,"* would not have impacted me so greatly. I would NOT have become intent on finding my own *"Jane"* for whom I could live *"happily ever after."* Ironically, Mother's lifelong misery was a blessing for me. Seeing her unhappiness, feeling it day after day, motivated me to become what I thought necessary to find my own *"soulmate!"* I believed, at six-years old, were I to become *"Tarzanesque"* in character, that'd be my best chance to find *"true love"* and *"happiness.."* And, in the end, it was...

The "IRISHMAN" & MOTHER & A CHIRSTMAS DANCE

The fighter pilot that'd become a Nicaraguan crop duster, a man six- foot four with pale green eyes and with hair the color of flame was ALSO a romantic, an adventurer, and the perfect *"Knight in Shining Armor"* Mother had sought her entire life. What follows is an anecdotal tale that of the Irishman's romantic character and Mother's destiny once we'd returned to America after the jungle plane crash.

It was winter in Kansas City, Missouri the month of Christmas, 1966 ~ less than four months after I'd survived the Nicaraguan plane crash. The Irishman had temporarily moved to Kansas City. The tale that follows occurred on a wintry day. A snowstorm was brewing:

On this day, we four, me, Mother, the Irishman, and his daughter had decided to eat at an illusory *"hamburger joint"* no one would ever suspect could make delectable exotic hamburgers. The place sat partially *"obumbrated"* within the hollow of a massive boulder that, 50,000 years ago, had been carried to this site at the edge of a glacial till. The owner of this place had converted an *"Airstream Silver Camper"* into a cozy place to eat ~ a renowned but still covert *"hamburger joint."*

By its revamped design, the *"camper"* had become a romantic, anachronistic place. Above a black and white checkered linoleum floor, both sides of the camper had been befitted with a row of circular silver bar stools cushioned by red vinyl seats that sat beneath a red acrylic counter the length of the camper. One side of the camper had a panoramic window through which could be viewed, past a park of ancient massive oak trees and a Greek fountain, the *"Country Club Plaza."* Through the arc of the giant oaks, the *"Plaza"* appeared as though it were a chimerically lit amphitheater; an enclave of Kansas City that emulated the architecture of Spain. During this late evening, as had been the case every Christmas season, it had been set aglow by thousands of Christmas lights and the red-green décor that of Santa's *"North Pole."*

On this day, the *"joint"* was empty. The weathermen had predicted a particularly threatening wintry storm.

So, most people that day did not venture from their homes let alone go to work. But mother had so gloriously described this place to the Irishman, he felt compelled to go there even on an evening such as this. He also felt it'd be more *"cozy"* than usual since it'd probably be deserted.

He was right. We were the ONLY people there. We ordered hamburgers and fries and a coke and nestled together upon our stools. As we sat looking out the panoramic window at a scene of wonderment, almost inaudibly, Mother and the Irishman began *"small talk"* woven with erogenous subtleties that blatantly suggested each was enamored with the other. My mother had an ingenious demure of seduction without seduction.

As we casually ate, the wind abruptly picked up. The branches of the oaks outside began flailing widely. Blustery snow came. Frost diffused and thickened across the panoramic window until only a fragment of sight could be seen through it. We began to worry. We decided we'd head home before the weather became impassable.

We left the *"camper"* after devouring every scrap of hamburger and French fry and forged our way through snow so thick we were forced to find the parked car essentially by *"braille."* Mother and the Irishman sat in the front seat. He drove. His daughter and me, we sat in the back seat. Kansas City was hilly and our journey toward home was fraught with numerous slides and misdirection. But slowly we continued onward unscathed…

The City of Kansas City, Missouri comes to a hilly pinnacle within a four-way convergence of stoplights whereat there had once been built its most prestigious stores. As we approached this pinnacle halfway to our destination toward home, the car's radio began playing a rerun of *"Can't Stop Loving You."* This was a song Elvis sang in his 1961 movie, *"Blue Hawaii."* There are songs that capture the soul. This song was one of those…

In a city once bustling with activity, the winter storm had besieged its streets ~ no soul, no vehicle was *"out and about"* save ours. It was as though the city had been abandoned in the wake of a snowy avalanche. Upon hearing *"Can't Stop Loving You,"* the Irishman gently pressed the brake of the car. We came sliding into the middle of the four-way stoplight at the very crest of the city. By the time we'd reached this intersection, night had made full its impact yet was softened to grey by the crystalline glimmer of the sky. Christmas lights were fully lit, and the snow had thickened to a foot of pillowy feathery fluff. Though it must have been very cold the wind had become still, and the snowflakes had taken to falling vertically, drifting downward ever so slowly as though cushioned by some fairytale charismatic force. Outside felt *"warm (?)."*

The strangest thing then happened…

The World War II Irish fighter pilot turned up the radio and stepped out of the car. Dumbfounded, I watched him circle the car to my mother's door. Opening her door, he held out a hand and asked her to dance. The two of them danced entwined in a romantic embrace until the song ended. Without a word between them, without more than the warmth of his lips gently pressed against her hand as the song ended, he brought her back to the car. In silence, we drove home…

Such idyllic interludes of romance came again and again, spontaneously conjured, spontaneously imagined by the fighter pilot. He enmeshed my mother in a world she'd long fantasized. Within the next year, mother divorced my second father, the pharmacist, and married the Irishman. He became my third father, the crop duster, and his daughter became my "*sister-in-law!*"

EPILOGUE

Before I set about writing how it came to be at age six I sought to become the avatar of *"Tarzan,"* I'd never realized this epic tale written within the imaginative scripts of Edgar Rice Burroughs' genius, exemplified the idea of synchronicity:

> Jane Porter, a woman of youth, naïve, delicate, coveted by wealth, with the blessings of her eccentric father, Archimedes Porter, a professor of science, sets sail toward the continent of Africa to land upon the shores of its most dangerous jungle. Within that jungle exists predation raw in tooth and fang and claw; primitives that eat human flesh, and a density of forest no maiden of that time would dare to journey.

> There, brachiating through trees at the edge of that vast continent almost twelve million square miles in size, there exists only one man, among 1.6 BILLION (the population of Earth in 1900 A.D.), suited perfectly for Jane; a man her percipient nature sees not as a sav-

age, stupid brute but as a being of character and exceptional quality ~ a man for which she will find indelible love. What are the odds were it not for the phenomena of synchronicity?

As I think about it, I find it almost magical, it took writing, many years later, about my plane crash within the wiles of Nicaragua, to realize the very novel that set me on the path of emulating a character I admired, *"Tarzan & His Mate,"* exemplified the phenomenon of synchronicity within the pages of Burroughs' epic...

END

GLOSSARY

CONCATENTATION: Linked, sequential events, delayed by intervals of time, but that are consequentially connected to dispatch the *"weave"* within the tapestry of life lived.

SYNCHRONICITY: Highly, astronomical improbable coincidental sequential events originating as acausal thought (dreams, desires, fantasies ~ all intangible) that become causal (become real; become tangible).

FATE: Infers a preordained, divine plan irrespective of human will (a Greek concept). Human morality, human responsibility cannot alter final outcomes; there is NO *"free will."*

DESTINY: Infers *"free will"* plays a part in the outcome of an individual's future. The future is not random. It is *"guided"* by choices made affected by human morality and human responsibility.

ROMANCE: By my definition romance MUST BE a novel, unique expression of love between two people. It cannot be bromidic or derived from social tropes that are uncreative and repetitive.

LOVE: Best defined in a book written by Erich Fromm entitled, "*The Art of Loving.*" In this book he delineates what MUST BE present for love to be everlasting: CARE, RESPECT, KNOWLEDGE; RESPON-SIBILITY. If these elements are missing, love will be ephemeral. As simple as it seems, it is a discipline hard to follow.